Contents

Introduction

Evaluation can be described as an attempt to analyse the learning that a pupil has achieved over a period of time as a result of the classroom teaching/learning situation. It plays an integral part in the teaching and learning process.

The evaluation material in this Test Booklet has been designed to analyse pupils' progress, with the aim of reinforcing the positive aspects and identifying areas for improvement.

There are five main reasons for evaluation:

Formative – to increase motivation by making evaluation a part of the continuous learning process.

Summative – to give pupils feedback on their progress or achievement at a particular point in time, often formally through tests.

Informative – to give pupils and parents feedback on progress or achievements.

Diagnostic – to monitor individual pupils' needs and help identify pupils who need special support.

Evaluative – to identify pupils' level of achievement and select or order pupils according to merit, to check effectiveness of teaching methods, teaching materials and teachers.

This Test Booklet contains one Placement test, eight Unit tests, three End of term tests, one Final test, and one Exam preparation test.

The Placement test can be used as a diagnostic test at the start of the year, reviewing learning from the previous year and helping to assess pupils' ability.

The Unit tests can be used at the end of each unit, to monitor pupils' progress through the course, to give pupils feedback on their achievement and to identify areas requiring reinforcement.

The End of term and Final tests can be used as informative and evaluative tests, for reporting purposes.

The Exam preparation test can be used to help prepare pupils for external exams such as CYLETS and Trinity.

A and B versions have been provided for the Unit tests, the Final test and the Exam preparation test. Both versions cover exactly the same learning objectives, and will provide an equal level of evaluation. You may find it useful to hand out different A and B versions to students who sit next to each other. Alternatively, you could use the A version to test the whole class and use the B version for reinforcement purposes.

The four skills of Reading, Writing, Listening and Speaking are tested through self-explanatory activities that students will be familiar with from their work in class.

Each activity has its own score, with a consolidated score at the end of each page and a total score at the end of each test. Points have been allocated according to the number of tasks pupils are required to do in each activity.

For Speaking activities, points have been allocated according to the learning objectives. In the lower levels of the course, points should be awarded for correct word identification. In the higher levels of the course, longer answers are expected, and points should be awarded for production of the target language. Pupils should be allowed to make more than one attempt, and you should encourage them to self-correct.

Procedure on the day before the evaluation

- Review unit content using games to give practice for the coming evaluation.
- Ask pupils to predict what they think the content of the evaluation might be, using L1 as needed.

Procedure on the day of evaluation

- Play a game, and sing a song or chant to help pupils to move from L1 to English.
- Play the audio and direct pupils to complete the listening activities. Audio files are available on the Active Teach, or at pearsonelt.com/islands.
- As with the audio throughout this course, you may wish to pause the audio to allow pupils to complete each question.
- Depending on your classroom setup, you may wish to set pupils up in pairs to complete the speaking activity and monitor the class as a whole. Alternatively, you may prefer to have pupils speak individually to you while the remainder of the class works through the reading and writing exercises.
- Have some small pieces of scrap paper available for students to make notes for their speaking evaluation. Emphasise that they only should make notes. Try to avoid full sentences or scripts being written.
- Set pupils a time limit within which to complete the remainder of the test.
- Pupils will need colouring pens or pencils for some of the activities.
- Check the answers against the Answer Key on pages 72–76. Please note that the answers for the speaking activities are intended as suggested answers only. Write the total score in the space provided at the bottom of each page and at the end of the tests.
- When handing tests back to pupils, go through the answers and explain any errors.

Poptropica English Islands also encourages the practice of self-evaluation, which is provided at the end of each unit in the Activity Book. This gives the pupils an important opportunity to express their own opinion about their progress in English.

1 Read and number. (4 points)

1 She's doing homework.
2 He's walking.
3 He's sleeping.
4 He's listening to music.

a  ☐   **b** ☐   **c** ☐   **d**  ☐

2 Read and circle. Then match. (12 points)

1 What (do / does) you like doing?
2 (Do / Does) Anna like peas?
3 Can he (run / running)?
4 (Has / Have) she got a round chin?
5 What are you (wear / wearing)?
6 What does (it / they) look like?

a No, she doesn't.
b I like playing the guitar.
c I'm wearing a blue a shirt.
d Yes, he can.
e It's got a tail and big ears.
f No, she hasn't.

3 Read and write *T = True* or *F = False*. (6 points)

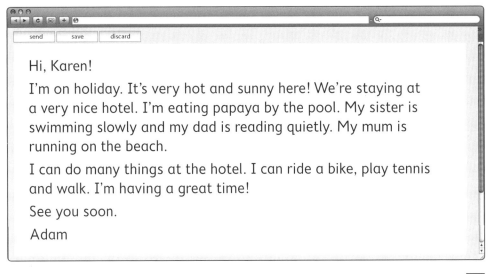

Hi, Karen!

I'm on holiday. It's very hot and sunny here! We're staying at a very nice hotel. I'm eating papaya by the pool. My sister is swimming slowly and my dad is reading quietly. My mum is running on the beach.

I can do many things at the hotel. I can ride a bike, play tennis and walk. I'm having a great time!

See you soon.

Adam

1 Adam is on holiday. ☐
2 It's cold and rainy. ☐
3 His sister is reading slowly. ☐
4 His mum is running on the beach. ☐
5 He can't ride a bike at the hotel. ☐
6 He can play tennis at the hotel. ☐

Score: ___ /22

1 Write. (6 points)

likes   younger   name   brother   nine   is

My ¹ _____ is Mary. I'm ² _____ years old.

This is my ³ _____ Rob. He ⁴ _____ six.

He's ⁵ _____ than me. He ⁶ _____ reading and writing!

2 Read and answer. (7 points)

1 When were you born? _____

2 Have you got brown hair? _____

3 Can you swim? _____

4 Are you writing? _____

5 What do you do after school? _____

6 Do you like peas? _____

7 Has your teacher got glasses? _____

3 Draw and write about your family. (6 points)

My family

There are _____ people in my family.

I've got _____

_____.

My _____ likes _____

_____.

_____

_____

_____

_____

_____

Score: ____ /19

Placement

  1 **Listen and write. (10 points)**

	Age	Favourite number	Hair colour	Favourite hobby
Alice	9			painting
Amy		62	blond	
Bill	10			
Tom			brown	

  2 **Listen and circle. (8 points)**

1 19 / 90   **2** 15 / 50   **3** 20 / 30   **4** 18 / 80
5 14 / 40   **6** 17 / 70   **7** 13 / 30   **8** 16 / 60

  3 **Listen and match. (8 points)**

1 Alice   **a** skiing   **e** every morning
2 Darren   **b** walking the dog   **f** after school
3 Jo   **c** cooking   **g** at the weekend
4 Alex   **d** chatting online   **h** in winter

4 **Look and say. (8 points)**

on	in	next to	opposite	behind	in front of	above	under

There is/are …

It's …

Score: ___ /34

Whole test score: ___ /75

1 Look and write. (4 points)

| 1 I don't like _____. | 2 Tom likes _____. | 3 They like _____. | 4 Anna doesn't like _____. |

2 Unscramble and write. (8 points)

1 _____? Henry / like / does / playing hockey
_____ (✓)

2 _____? she / like / skipping / does
_____ (✗)

3 _____? like / do / skiing / your grandparents
_____ (✗)

4 _____? do / like / you / surfing the internet
_____ (✓)

3 Read and write. (7 points)

playing   like   magazines   dog   cooking   guitar   doing

Donna: What do you like [1] _____, Emily?

Emily: I like walking my [2] _____ and I like [3] _____ hockey with my friends.

Donna: And what do you like doing with your family?

Emily: I like singing and playing the [4] _____ with my family. What about you, Donna?

Donna: I like reading [5] _____. My dad likes [6] _____. He makes great burgers and pancakes!

Emily: I [7] _____ cooking with my mum. We like painting and drawing, too.

4 Write about what you like and don't like doing. (6 points)

I like _____.   I don't like _____.
_____   _____
_____   _____
_____   _____

Score: ___ /25

Free time

1 **Listen and circle. (4 points)**

1 Robert likes
  a skiing.
  b skateboarding.
  c riding his scooter.

2 Daisy likes
  a playing football.
  b reading magazines.
  c reading books.

3 Jack likes
  a playing the guitar.
  b playing football.
  c watching TV.

4 Pat likes
  a cooking.
  b painting.
  c watching TV.

2 **Listen and tick (✓) or cross (✗). (5 points)**

1 Tom likes running. ☐

2 Jo and Sue like painting pictures of animals. ☐

3 Charlie doesn't like playing football. ☐

4 Val doesn't like reading magazines. ☐

5 Tony likes riding his scooter. ☐

3 **Draw things your friends like and don't like doing. Then say. (6 points)**

like	don't like

What does he/she like doing?

He/She likes/doesn't like …

Do they like …?

Score: ___ /15

Whole test score: ___ /40

1 Look and write. (4 points)

1 I don't like	2 Anna likes	3 Sally doesn't like	4 Tony likes
_____.	_____.	_____.	_____.

2 Unscramble and write. (8 points)

1 _____? Willie / walking the dog / like / does
  _____ (✗)

2 _____? you / do / like / surfing the internet
  _____ (✓)

3 _____? riding a scooter / Cindy / does / like
  _____ (✗)

4 _____? like / painting / they / do
  _____ (✓)

3 Read and write. (7 points)

> likes   don't   like   playing   TV   cooking   chatting

At the weekend I [1] _____ skateboarding and playing hockey with my friends.
I also like [2] _____ online and [3] _____ computer games.
They're so much fun! I [4] _____ like watching [5] _____ at the
weekend but my brother does. He [6] _____ watching TV in his bedroom.
On Sundays we like [7] _____ together. We make a big lunch with salad
and vegetables.

4 Write about what your friend likes and doesn't like doing. (6 points)

He/She likes _____.   He/She doesn't like _____.
_____   _____
_____   _____
_____   _____

Score: ____ /25

1 **Listen and circle. (4 points)**

1 Robert likes
  a riding his scooter.
  b skiing.
  c skateboarding.
3 Jack likes
  a watching TV.
  b playing football.
  c playing the guitar.

2 Daisy likes
  a reading magazines.
  b reading books.
  c playing football.
4 Pat likes
  a watching TV.
  b cooking.
  c painting.

2 **Listen and tick (✓) or cross (✗). (5 points)**

1 Tom likes skipping. ☐

2 Jo and Sue don't like painting pictures of flowers. ☐

3 Charlie likes playing football. ☐

4 Val loves reading magazines. ☐

5 Tony doesn't like riding bikes. ☐

3 **Draw what you like and don't like doing. Then say. (6 points)**

like	don't like

What do you like doing?

I like/don't like ...

Do you like ...?

Score: ___ /15

Whole test score: ___ /40

1 Unscramble and write. Then number. (8 points)

1 dpnaa _____   2 kmenyo _____

3 amet _____   4 irfut _____

a [ ]   **b** [ ]   **c** [ ]   **d** [ ]

2 Unscramble and write. (5 points)

1 hippos / eat / do / what

_____ ?

2 do / where / live / camels

_____ ?

3 live / lions / where / do

_____ ?

4 eat / do / what / giraffes

_____ ?

5 what / eat / crocodiles / do

_____ ?

3 Read and circle. (5 points)

1 How (much / many) teeth have they got?
2 How (much / many) fruit do monkeys eat?
3 Giraffes (has / have) got 32 teeth.
4 Monkeys (eat / eats) fruit.
5 Zebras (run fast / fast run).

4 Write about an animal. (6 points)

_____ live in _____ .
They've got _____ .
They eat _____ .
They can _____ .

Score: ____ /24

1 **Listen and circle. (4 points)**

1 (a)    (b)   (c)

2 (a)    (b)    (c)

3 (a)    (b)    (c)

4 (a)   (b)   (c)

2 **Listen and tick (✓) the words you hear. (6 points)**

hippo ☐	rainforests ☐	monkey ☐	crocodile ☐	panda ☐
forest ☐	river ☐	giraffe ☐	elephant ☐	zebra ☐
desert ☐	camel ☐	lion ☐	crab ☐	grasslands ☐

3 **Choose an animal and say. (6 points)**

1    2   3

Where does it live?

Can it ... fast/well?

What does it eat?

How much/many ...?

Score: ___ /16

Whole test score: ___ /40

1 Unscramble and write. Then number. (8 points)

1 pihop _____   **2** veslae _____

3 regfaif _____   **4** srags _____

a [ ]   **b** [ ]   **c** [ ]   **d** [ ]

2 Unscramble and write. (5 points)

1 do / live / zebras / where

_____?

2 eat / pandas / what / do

_____?

3 crocodiles / do / where / live

_____?

4 do / what / eat / birds

_____?

5 gorillas / live / where / do

_____?

3 Read and circle. (5 points)

1 How (much / many) meat do lions eat?

2 Fish (swim well / well swim).

3 How (much / many) teeth have cats got?

4 Zebras (live / living) in grasslands.

5 They eat (a lot / fast) of leaves.

4 Write about an animal. (6 points)

_____ live in _____.

They've got _____.

They eat _____.

They can _____.

Score: ___ /24

2 **Wild animals**

Listening and speaking B

1 🎧 07 **Listen and circle. (4 points)**

1 (a)   (b)    (c)

2 (a)    (b)    (c)

3 (a)    (b)    (c)

4 (a)   (b)    (c)

2 🎧 08 **Listen and tick (✓) the words you hear. (6 points)**

rainforests ☐	forest ☐	crocodile ☐	grasslands ☐	elephant ☐
river ☐	crab ☐	lion ☐	zebra ☐	giraffe ☐
hippo ☐	desert ☐	monkey ☐	panda ☐	camel ☐

3 **Choose an animal and say. (6 points)**

(1)    (2)    (3)

Where does it live?

Can it ... fast/well?

What does it eat?

How much/many ...?

Score: ___ /16

Whole test score: ___ /40

1 **Look and write. (6 points)**

 1 _____

 2 _____

 3 _____

 4 _____

 5 _____

 6 _____

2 **Unscramble and write. (4 points)**

1 like / what / the / last / weather / summer / was

_____?

2 weather / today / what's / the / like

_____?

3 yesterday / what / the / was / temperature

_____?

4 temperature / the / today / what's

_____?

3 **Read and write *T = True* or *F = False*. (6 points)**

Chris goes hiking in autumn. He loves looking at the leaves. Ben goes water skiing in summer when the water is warm. Jane and Liz go snowboarding in winter. They go every year in January. Alice and Michelle go camping in spring. They like the flowers.

1 Ben goes hiking in autumn. ☐

2 Chris loves looking at the leaves. ☐

3 Ben goes surfing in summer. ☐

4 Jane and Liz don't go snowboarding in winter. ☐

5 Alice and Michelle don't go camping in spring. ☐

6 Alice and Michelle like the flowers. ☐

4 **Write about what you do in each season. (6 points)**

I go _____

_____. (autumn)

I _____

_____. (summer)

Score: ___ /22

Listen and circle. (4 points)

1 The weather is

  a cold and stormy.

  b warm and wet.

  c humid with thunder.

3 Today there's

  a lightning and rain.

  b a lot of wind.

  c not much rain.

2 The temperature is about

  a 33 degrees.

  b 23 degrees.

  c 25 degrees.

4 It's about

  a 31 degrees.

  b 11 degrees.

  c 21 degrees.

 Listen, match and write. (8 points)

1 Jim and Claire go

2 Carol goes

3 Pete and Nick go

4 Pat and Helen go

  a snowboarding in _____.

  b water skiing in _____.

  c camping in _____.

  d hiking in _____.

Look at the picture and say. (6 points)

What was the weather like/the temperature?

What does she do in ...?

What do you do in ...?

Score: ___ /18

Whole test score: ___ /40

1 **Look and write. (6 points)**

①
_____

②
_____

③
_____

④
_____

⑤
_____

⑥
_____

2 **Unscramble and write. (4 points)**

1 today / weather / what's / like / the

_____?

2 temperature / today / what's / the

_____?

3 was / temperature / the / what / yesterday

_____?

4 weather / last / what / the / was / week / like

_____?

3 **Read and write _T = True_ or _F = False_. (6 points)**

Sally and Tom go snowboarding in winter. They like snowy days! Jack goes hiking in the mountains. He goes in spring when it's warm. Emma goes water skiing in summer. She goes water skiing on a lake. She likes swimming. George and Ben go camping in summer. They like sleeping under the stars.

1 Sally and Tom go hiking in winter. ☐

2 Sally doesn't like snowy days. ☐

3 Jack goes hiking when it's warm. ☐

4 Emma goes water skiing in summer. ☐

5 Emma likes swimming. ☐

6 George and Ben go camping in autumn. ☐

4 **Write about what you do in each season. (6 points)**

I go _____

_____. (spring)

I _____

_____. (winter)

Score: ____ /22

1   **Listen and circle. (4 points)**

1 The weather is
   a warm and wet.
   b cold and stormy.
   c humid with lightning.

3 Today there's
   a a lot of wind.
   b not much rain.
   c thunder and rain.

2 The temperature is about
   a 23 degrees.
   b 25 degrees.
   c 33 degrees.

4 It's about
   a 11 degrees.
   b 21 degrees.
   c 31 degrees.

2 **Listen, match and write. (8 points)**

1 Jim and Claire go
2 Carol goes
3 Pete and Nick go
4 Pat and Helen go

a water skiing in _____.
b hiking in _____.
c snowboarding in _____.
d camping in _____.

3 **Look at the picture and say. (6 points)**

What was the weather like/the temperature?

What does he do in ...?

What do you do in ...?

Score: ___ /18

Whole test score: ___ /40

1 **Read and match. (4 points)**

1 What do you do on Thursdays?	**a** He studies English at 11 o'clock.
2 What does Jenny do on Fridays?	**b** I practise the violin.
3 When do you learn to cook?	**c** I learn to cook on Sundays.
4 When does he study English?	**d** She learns to draw.

2 **Read and circle. (4 points)**

When do you have music lessons, Bob?

I have music lessons on Mondays at 10.00. When do you have music lessons, Sue?

I have music lessons on Wednesdays at 2:45. When does Frankie do karate?

Frankie does karate at 3.30.

1 Bob and Sue (have music lessons / do gymnastics).

2 Bob has music lessons on Monday (afternoons / mornings).

3 Sue has music lessons at (quarter to three / quarter past three).

4 Frankie does karate at (half past four / half past three).

3 **Unscramble and write. (4 points)**

1 the / always / Jane / has / piano / lessons / in / morning

_____.

2 Henry / do / gymnastics / does / when

_____?

3 midday / to / my brother / often / learns / at / cook

_____.

4 on / does / what / Saturdays / she / do

_____?

4 **Write about your week. (5 points)**

On Mondays _____.

On _____.

_____

_____

Score: ____ /17

1 🎧 **Listen and write. (5 points)**

1 Jenny practises the _____ on Wednesdays.

2 She has ballet lessons on Sunday _____.

3 She learns to draw on Friday _____.

4 She _____ English on Tuesday evenings.

5 She does gymnastics on _____.

2 🎧 **Listen and match. (12 points)**

1 have ballet lessons	every day	12.00
2 study Maths	Mondays	11.30
3 learn to cook	Saturday afternoons	3.15
4 do karate	every morning	6.45
5 practise the violin	Wednesday afternoons	4.00
6 learn to draw	Tuesday evenings	6.30

3 **Make some notes about the activities you do. Then say. (6 points)**

Activity	Day	When

What activities do you do?

What do you do on ...?

When do you ...?

Score: ____ /23

Whole test score: ____ /40

1 **Read and match. (4 points)**

1 When do you have ballet lessons?
2 What does your brother do on Mondays?
3 When does Sarah learn to draw?
4 What do you do on Saturdays?

a I have ballet lessons on Tuesdays.
b I practise the violin.
c He learns to cook.
d She learns to draw at 10 o'clock.

2 **Read and circle. (4 points)**

When do you do gymnastics, Charlie?

I do gymnastics on Tuesdays at 10:45. When does Tim have music lessons?

I do gymnastics on Thursdays at 4.00. When do you do gymnastics, Helen?

Tim has music lessons on Saturdays at 5.30.

1 Charlie and Helen (have music lessons / do gymnastics).
2 Charlie does gymnastics on Thursday (afternoons / mornings).
3 Helen does gymnastics at (quarter to ten / quarter to eleven).
4 Tim has music lessons at (half past five / half past three).

3 **Unscramble and write. (4 points)**

1 practise / do / the / when / you / piano

_____?

2 often / my sister / English / studies / afternoon / in / the

_____.

3 karate / Jack / four / does / o'clock / at

_____.

4 to / when / learn / does / he / draw

_____?

4 **Write about your weekends. (5 points)**

On Saturdays _____.
On _____.

_____

Score: ___ /17

4 My week

 Listen and write. (5 points)

1 Jenny _____ the piano on Wednesdays after school.

2 She has her ballet lessons on _____ mornings.

3 She learns to _____ on Friday afternoons.

4 She studies English on Tuesday _____.

5 She does _____ on Saturdays.

 Listen and match. (12 points)

1 have ballet lessons	Wednesday afternoons	3.15
2 study Maths	Saturday afternoons	12.00
3 learn to cook	Tuesday evenings	4.00
4 do karate	every morning	11.30
5 practise the violin	Mondays	6.45
6 learn to draw	every day	6.30

3 **Make some notes about the activities your family member does. Then say. (6 points)**

Activity	Day	When

What activities does he/she do?

What does he/she do on ...?

When does he/she ...?

Score: ____ /23

Whole test score: ____ /40

1 Look and write. (6 points)

① _____

② _____

③ _____

④ _____

⑤ _____

⑥ _____

2 Read and write. Then match. (8 points)

1 _____ do you want to be?

2 What _____ Tina want to be?

3 _____ Helena want to be a singer?

4 Do you _____ to be a film star?

a Yes, she does. She loves singing.

b I want to be a mechanic.

c She wants to be a firefighter.

d No, I don't. I want to be an astronaut.

3 Read and write. (4 points)

| jump   basketball player   helps   want |

I ^{1} _____ to be in the Olympic Games. I want to be a ^{2} _____ because I can ^{3} _____ high and run fast. I always train at six o'clock in the morning before going to school. My coach is named Wendy. She ^{4} _____ me a lot.

4 What does your friend want to be? Why? Draw and write. (6 points)

He/She wants to be _____ .

_____

_____

_____

_____

_____

Score: ____ /24

①   **Listen and circle. (4 points)**

1 Sally wants to be a (firefighter / ballet dancer).

2 Dan (wants to be / doesn't want to be) a police officer.

3 Pat wants to be a (journalist / police officer).

4 Ben wants to be a (builder / film star).

② **Read and write T = True or F = False. (6 points)**

1 Jim doesn't want to be a carpenter. ☐

2 Paul wants to be a carpenter. ☐

3 Karen wants to be a model. ☐

4 Simon wants to be a film star. ☐

5 Lucy wants to be a photographer. ☐

6 Pam doesn't want to be an athlete. ☐

③ **Make notes about what you want and don't want to be. Then say. (6 points)**

want to be	why

don't want to be	why not

What do you want to be?

I want to be a/an … because …

Do you want to be a/an …?

I don't want to be a/an … because …

Score: ___ /16

Whole test score: ___ /40

1 **Look and write. (6 points)**

1 _____

2 _____

3 _____

4 _____

5 _____

6 _____

2 **Read and write. Then match. (8 points)**

1 What _____ you want to be?

2 What _____ he want to be?

3 Does Jane _____ to be a photographer?

4 Do you want to _____ a model?

a No, I don't.

b I want to be a journalist.

c He wants to be a mechanic.

d No, she doesn't.

3 **Read and write. (4 points)**

| lessons don't practise because |

I ^{1} _____ want to be a doctor or an astronaut. I want to be a famous singer
^{2} _____ I can sing very well. I can play the piano, too. I have piano
^{3} _____ on Tuesdays and Thursdays. I always ^{4} _____
in the afternoon.

4 **What do you want to be? Why? Draw and write. (6 points)**

I want to be _____.

_____

_____

_____

_____

_____

Score: ____ /24

5 Jobs

1 **Listen and circle. (4 points)**

1 Sally (wants to be / doesn't want to be) a ballet dancer.

2 Dan doesn't want to be a (police officer / film star).

3 Pat wants to be a (police officer / journalist).

4 Ben (wants to be / doesn't want to be) a film star.

2 **Read and write T = True or F = False. (6 points)**

1 Jim wants to be a carpenter. ☐

2 Paul doesn't want to be a carpenter. ☐

3 Karen wants to be a lawyer. ☐

4 Simon wants to be a singer. ☐

5 Lucy wants to be an athlete. ☐

6 Pam doesn't want to be an astronaut. ☐

3 **Make notes about what your friend wants and doesn't want to be. Then say. (6 points)**

wants to be	why

doesn't want to be	why not

What does he/she want to be?

He/She wants to be a/an ... because ...

Does he/she want to be a/an ...?

He/She doesn't want to be a/an ... because ...

Score: ____ /16

Whole test score: ____ /40

1 **Unscramble and write. Then number. (8 points)**

1 snive _____
2 tens _____
3 eyallv _____
4 ebrdig _____

a b c d

☐ ☐ ☐ ☐

2 **Read and write. (6 points)**

I'm on holiday in the rainforest. Yesterday morning I ¹ _____ (walk) through
the valley near my hut and I ² _____ (look) at the colourful flowers.
I ³ _____ (listen) to a hummingbird in a tree. I ⁴ _____ (climb) the tree but
I could not see the hummingbird. In the afternoon it was very humid. I ⁵ _____ (stay)
in the hut and ⁶ _____ (play) with my friend.

3 **Unscramble and write. (4 points)**

1 2 3 4

1 hills / could / towards / they / go / the _____ ?
2 walk / he / the / could / mountain / around _____ ?
3 could / around / the / walk / lake / she _____ ?
4 river / he / swim / could / the / through _____ ?

4 **Draw your favourite rainforest animal and write. (6 points)**

My favourite _____

_____.

I like them because _____

_____.

They've got _____

_____.

They live _____

_____.

They eat _____

_____.

Score: ___ /24

Poptropica English Islands – Test Booklet 4
PHOTOCOPIABLE

Listen and write. (6 points)

1 First she walks on the path and goes _____ the bridge.

2 Then she goes _____ the mountain.

3 After that she walks next to a small river. Then she walks _____ the river.

4 Next she walks _____ the lake.

5 And then she walks past a beautiful _____.

6 After the waterfall she goes over the _____. Then she can see her hut.

 Listen and circle. (4 points)

1 They could run (over / around) a mountain.

2 There was a big (tapir / tarantula) behind their hut.

3 They (could / couldn't) hear the birds.

4 They could see the (sea / lake).

3 **Look at the picture and imagine you were on the island yesterday. Then say. (6 points)**

There was/There were …

It was/They were …

I could/couldn't …

I walked/looked at …

Score: ___ /16

Whole test score: ___ /40

1 **Unscramble and write. Then number. (8 points)**

1 afwetallr _____
2 snive _____
3 tens _____
4 ntainoum _____

a □ b □ c □ d □

2 **Read and write. (6 points)**

I'm having a great time! Yesterday morning I ¹ _____ (hike) through the rainforest and I ² _____ (climb) up to a waterfall. There were some boys there. One of them ³ _____ (jump) from the top of the waterfall! In the afternoon I ⁴ _____ (walk) near our huts with my brother. We ⁵ _____ (look) for a giant tarantula and we ⁶ _____ (play) with a small monkey.

3 **Unscramble and write. (4 points)**

1 □ 2 □ 3 □ 4 □

1 river / he / swim / could / the / through _____?
2 hills / could / towards / they / go / the _____?
3 walk / he / the / could / mountain / around _____?
4 could / around / the / walk / lake / she _____?

4 **Draw your favourite rainforest animal and write. (6 points)**

My favourite _____
_____.
I like them because _____
_____.
They've got _____
_____.
They live _____
_____.
They eat _____
_____.

Score: ____ /24

© **Pearson** Education Limited 2017 PHOTOCOPIABLE

1 **Listen and write. (6 points)**

1 First she goes on a path and goes across the _____.

2 Then she goes around a big _____.

3 After that she walks next to a small river. Then she walks _____ the river.

4 Next she walks towards the _____.

5 And then she walks _____ a waterfall.

6 Lastly, she goes _____ the hill. Then she can see her hut.

2 **Listen and circle. (4 points)**

1 They could run (around / over) a mountain.

2 There was a big (tarantula / tapir) behind their hut.

3 They (could / couldn't) see the birds.

4 They couldn't see the (lake / sea).

3 **Look at the picture and imagine you were on the island yesterday. Then say. (6 points)**

There was/There were …

It was/They were …

I could/couldn't …

I walked/looked at …

Score: ___ /16

Whole test score: ___ /40

1 Look and write. (4 points)

①   ②   ③   ④

He's _____.   She's _____.   He's _____.   She's _____.

2 Read and match. (5 points)

1   What's the matter?
2   How do you feel?
3   What makes you feel relaxed?
4   Why are you crying?
5   It's John's birthday.

a   Watching TV.
b   I'm tired.
c   Give him some cake.
d   I feel happy.
e   Because I'm sad.

3 Read and write T = True or F = False. (5 points)

Dan: What's the matter, Kate? Why are you crying?
Kate: I'm sad.
Dan: Why are you sad?
Kate: I'm sad because I can't find my hamster.
Dan: Oh, no. I can help you find him. Look! He's under the sofa.
Kate: Get that box! We can catch him.
Dan: I've got him!

1   Kate is crying. ☐
2   Kate isn't sad. ☐
3   Dan can't find his hamster. ☐
4   The hamster is under the sofa. ☐
5   They haven't got a box. ☐

4 Write about what makes you feel happy and why. (6 points)

_____

_____

_____

_____

_____

_____

Score: ____ /20

1 **Listen and match. (6 points)**

1	Barry	**a**	is tired.
2	Helen	**b**	feels embarrassed.
3	James	**c**	isn't happy.
4	Sonia	**d**	feels nervous.
5	Gary	**e**	is worried.
6	Cindy	**f**	feels relieved.

2 **Listen and circle. (8 points)**

Al

1 He is (worried / proud) about his homework.

2 He was (tired / embarrassed) last night.

3 His mum was (angry / surprised).

4 He now feels more (relaxed / nervous).

Brenda

1 She's (angry / sad).

2 Her brother is (nervous / worried).

3 She was (surprised / nervous).

4 Her parents are (relieved / relaxed).

3 **Draw two pictures of yourself and talk about how you feel in each. (6 points)**

How do you feel?

Why are you ...?

I feel ...

I'm ... because ...

Score: ___ /20

Whole test score: ___ /40

1 Look and write. (4 points)

1 He's _____. 2 He's _____. 3 He's _____. 4 She's _____.

2 Read and match. (5 points)

1 The dog is hungry.
2 Emma is crying.
3 What makes you feel sad?
4 Why are you yawning?
5 How do you feel?

a I feel ill.
b Give her a hug.
c Rainy and cloudy days.
d Give him some food.
e Because I'm bored.

3 Read and write T = True or F = False. (5 points)

Jack: What's the matter, Pete?
Pete: I'm worried. I've got my Maths test later. Can you help me?
Jack: Yes! How do you feel?
Pete: Very nervous.
Jack: What makes you feel relaxed?
Pete: When I go for a walk.
Jack: We can take a walk by the lake …
Pete: Yes, a walk is a good idea.

1 Pete isn't worried. ☐
2 Jack can help him. ☐
3 Pete feels nervous. ☐
4 Pete feels relaxed when he goes for a walk. ☐
5 Jack can't go for a walk. ☐

4 Write about what makes you feel relaxed and why. (6 points)

_____
_____
_____
_____
_____
_____

Score: ___ /20

Listen and match. (6 points)

1	Barry	**a**	feels embarrassed.
2	Helen	**b**	is worried.
3	James	**c**	feels relieved.
4	Sonia	**d**	feels nervous.
5	Gary	**e**	is tired.
6	Cindy	**f**	isn't happy.

  Listen and circle. (8 points)

Al

1 He is (proud / worried) about his homework.

2 He was (embarrassed / tired) last night.

3 His mum was (surprised / angry).

4 He now feels more (nervous / relaxed).

Brenda

1 She's (sad / angry).

2 Her brother is (worried / nervous).

3 She was (nervous / surprised).

4 Her parents are (relaxed / tired).

3 **Draw two pictures of yourself and talk about how you feel in each. (6 points)**

How do you feel?

Why are you ...?

I feel ...

I'm ... because ...

Score: ____ /20

Whole test score: ____ /40

1 **Unscramble and write. Then number. (8 points)**

1 solnnlirkge _____
2 knaykagi _____
3 ihisnfg _____
4 snliiga _____

a
b
c
d

2 **Read and circle. (4 points)**

Hi. I'm Jo. I live near the sea and I love surfing. In summer, I go surfing with my friends every weekend. I've got a new surfboard. It's white and red. In autumn, I'm fond of kayaking on the sea. I've got a kayak, a paddle and a life jacket. My kayak and my surfboard are in a hut in my garden. I also often go horse-riding but I'm bored with it now. I want to do something new. My friends go rock climbing but I'm terrified of rock climbing. I love water sports and there's a river near my house. Maybe I can try rafting!

1 a Jo loves snorkelling.
  b Jo loves surfing.
  c Jo loves sailing.

3 a She hasn't got a paddle.
  b She has got a kayak.
  c She hasn't got a hut in her garden.

2 a She goes surfing in the morning.
  b She goes surfing every afternoon.
  c She goes surfing with her friends.

4 a Jo is terrified of rock climbing.
  b Jo is bored with rock climbing.
  c Jo is crazy about rock climbing.

3 **Unscramble and write. (8 points)**

1 _____? are / what / you / fond of
  _____. fond of / rafting / I'm
2 _____? got / a paddle / have / you
  _____. (✔)
3 _____! let's / bungee jumping / go
  _____. like / I / sorry, / bungee jumping / don't
4 _____? you / riding boots / got / have
  _____. (✗)

4 **Think of a weekend holiday. Then write about what you're going to do. (6 points)**

On Saturday I'm going to _____.
On _____.
_____.

Score: ____ /26

© Pearson Education Limited 2017 PHOTOCOPIABLE

1 🎧 19 **Listen and write T = True or F = False. (4 points)**

1 Eileen likes fishing with her mum. ☐

2 Eileen's scared of swimming under the water. ☐

3 Her brother is terrified of bungee jumping. ☐

4 Eileen is crazy about sailing. ☐

2 🎧 20 **Listen and tick (✓). (4 points)**

	rock climbing	fishing	snorkelling	beach volleyball	sailing	bungee jumping
1 bored with						
2 terrified of						
3 scared of						
4 crazy about						

3 **Look at the activities. Then talk about what you're *crazy about*, *scared of* and *bored with*. (6 points)**

 What are you ...?

I'm crazy about ...

I'm bored with ...

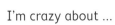 I'm scared of ...

Score: ____ /14

Whole test score: ____ /40

1 **Unscramble and write. Then number. (8 points)**

1 ifhgisn _____

2 srknolielgn _____

3 kagynkia _____

4 fsinrgu _____

(a) (b) (c) (d)

2 **Read and circle. (4 points)**

Hi. I'm Fran. I live next to a river in a forest. There are lots of hills and valleys in the forest. In spring, I often go rafting on the river with my friend, Val. We've got life jackets and paddles. My dad loves fishing and goes fishing on the river. In summer, I go horse-riding through the forest. I go with my brother and sister. We've got three small horses. We've also got riding hats and riding boots. We're crazy about riding. In autumn, my brother and sister go rock climbing in the mountains. I'm fond of walking in the mountains but I'm not fond of rock climbing. I'm scared of it.

1 **a** Fran often goes rafting in autumn.
   b Fran often goes rafting in spring.
   c Fran often goes rafting with her dad.

2 **a** Her dad goes fishing on the river.
   b Her dad hasn't got a fishing rod.
   c Her dad is bored with fishing.

3 **a** Her brother and sister go rock climbing in the mountains.
   b Her brother and sister go fishing.
   c Her brother and sister are scared of the mountains.

4 **a** Fran is scared of rivers.
   b Fran is fond of rock climbing.
   c Fran is scared of rock climbing.

3 **Unscramble and write. (8 points)**

1 _____! go / snorkelling / let's
   _____. don't / I / like / sorry, / snorkelling

2 _____? you / riding boots / got / have
   _____. (✗)

3 _____? are / what / you / fond of
   _____. fond of / rafting / I'm

4 _____? got / a life jacket / you / have
   _____. (✓)

4 **Think of a week holiday. Then write about what you're going to do. (6 points)**

On Monday I'm going to _____.
On _____.
_____.

Score: ___ /26

1 **Listen and write T = True or F = False. (4 points)**

1 Eileen is bored with fishing. ☐

2 Eileen's fond of scuba diving. ☐

3 She is terrified of bungee jumping. ☐

4 Eileen is scared of sailing. ☐

2 **Listen and tick (✓). (4 points)**

	snorkelling	beach volleyball	sailing	rock climbing	bungee jumping	fishing
1 bored with						
2 terrified of						
3 scared of						
4 crazy about						

3 **Look at the activities. Then talk about what you're _crazy about_, _scared of_ and _bored with_. (6 points)**

What are you ...?

I'm crazy about ...

I'm bored with ...

I'm scared of ...

Score: ___ /14

Whole test score: ___ /40

1 Read and match. (8 points)

1	What do you like doing?	a	Yes, they do.
2	What do your brother and sister like doing?	b	It was wet and warm.
3	Does Dan like playing hockey?	c	They like painting.
4	Do monkeys eat fruit?	d	No, he doesn't.
5	What do crabs eat?	e	They've got 32.
6	How many teeth have gorillas got?	f	It's stormy.
7	What's the weather like today?	g	I like skiing.
8	What was the weather like yesterday?	h	They eat worms.

2 Read and draw. (4 points)

1 Sally is taller than Tim. Sally likes painting. Tim likes playing the guitar.

2 It's stormy. There's lightning and thunder.

3 Pandas live in forests. They eat leaves.

4 I go camping in spring with my mum and dad. We like walking in the forest.

3 Read and write. (6 points)

1 What do you like doing at the weekend? _____

2 Do you like painting? _____

3 Where do camels live? _____

4 Do giraffes eat fish? _____

5 What's the temperature today? _____

6 What was the weather like yesterday? _____

Score: ____ /18

4 **Look and write. (6 points)**

1

2

3

_____

_____

_____

4

5

6

go _____

go_____

go_____

5 **Read and write. (12 points)**

> thunder   desert   grassland   autumn   summer   rainforest   warm
> humid   spring   degrees   forest   winter

Weather	Habitats	Seasons

6 **Write about what you and your family like doing. (8 points)**

| I like/don't like ...   My ... likes/doesn't like ... |

Free time

_____

_____

_____

_____

_____

_____

Score: ____ /26

7 **Listen and circle. (4 points)**

1 Sandy likes
   a chatting online.
   b playing computer games.
   c playing football.

3 Mary likes
   a skiing.
   b chatting online.
   c skateboarding.

2 Fred doesn't like
   a reading magazines.
   b watching the TV.
   c playing the guitar.

4 Matt likes
   a playing computer games.
   b watching films.
   c cooking.

8 **Listen and write. (4 points)**

Student's name: _____John_____

Favourite animals: **1** _____

Why? **2** They can _____. They're black and white.

What / eat: **3** _____

Where / live: **4** in _____

9 **Look. Then ask and answer. (7 points)**

What do you like doing?

Do you like ...?

Do your friends like ...?

Score: ____ /15

10 **Listen and write. (8 points)**

		Activity	Season
1	Tom		
2	Sally and Lisa		
3	John and George		
4	Mary		

11 **Listen and write T = True or F = False. (5 points)**

1 Anna's favourite animal likes sleeping all day. ☐

2 Rob likes living in his house. ☐

3 At the moment, the temperature is 5 degrees. ☐

4 Lisa doesn't like watching films with her brother. ☐

5 These animals eat leaves and fruits. ☐

12 **Draw yourself doing something in winter and say. (8 points)**

> What do you like doing?

> What's the weather like/ the temperature?

> What do you like doing in spring/ summer/autumn/winter?

Score: ___ /21

Whole test score: ___ /80

1 Read and match. (8 points)

1	What do you do on Thursdays?	a	Yes, I do.
2	When does Rosie have ballet lessons?	b	He wants to be a builder.
3	Does she want to be a lawyer?	c	It's past the waterfall.
4	Do you want to be a builder?	d	On Fridays at half past four.
5	Why do you want to be a carpenter?	e	No, we couldn't.
6	Where's your hut?	f	I do karate.
7	Could you go through the forest?	g	Because I like making chairs.
8	What does Harry want to be?	h	No, she doesn't.

2 Read and draw. (4 points)

1 Tim has ballet lessons.	**2** Charlie wants to be a basketball player.	**3** The monkey is near the hut.	**4** I could swim across the lake.

3 Read and write. (6 points)

1 What do you do on Sundays?

2 When do you study Maths?

3 Could you walk to school this morning?

4 Do you want to be a film star?

5 What do you want to be? Why?

6 Where's your school?

Score: ___ /18

End of term 2

4 **Look and write. (6 points)**

1 _____

2 _____

3 _____

4 _____

5 _____

6 _____

5 **Read and write. (12 points)**

over   nest   firefighter   across   waterfall   model   towards   vines   hut
around   astronaut   singer

Rainforest	Prepositions	Jobs
_____	_____	_____
_____	_____	_____
_____	_____	_____
_____	_____	_____

6 **Write about your week. (8 points)**

have   learn to   study   practise   in   on   at   quarter past   half past   quarter to

My week

On Mondays _____.

On _____.

_____

_____

_____

_____

_____

Score: ____ /26

7 Listen and match. (6 points)

| Mondays | Tuesdays | Wednesdays | Thursdays | Fridays | Saturdays |

8 Listen and write. (5 points)

1 Dan wants to be a(n) _____.

2 Ann wants to be a(n) _____.

3 Tim doesn't want to be a(n) _____.

4 Rob wants to be a(n) _____.

5 Claire doesn't want to be a(n) _____.

9 Read and draw. Then say. (7 points)

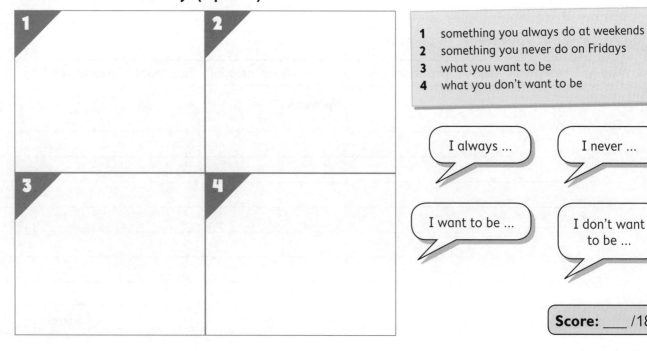

| 1 | 2 |
| 3 | 4 |

1 something you always do at weekends
2 something you never do on Fridays
3 what you want to be
4 what you don't want to be

I always …

I never …

I want to be …

I don't want to be …

Score: ___ /18

End of term 2

10 **Listen and write T = True or F = False. (6 points)**

1 The vines were past a small waterfall. ☐

2 They walked under a bridge. ☐

3 They could swim across a river. ☐

4 There was a lake between the forest and the hills. ☐

5 They weren't near the mountains. ☐

6 There weren't hummingbird nests near their hut. ☐

11 **Listen and circle. (6 points)**

1 At weekends, David (often / always) practises the violin.
David wants to be a (photographer / singer).

2 Sally couldn't (climb / hike) up the mountain.
They walked through a (forest / valley).

3 Jenny practises the piano on (Tuesdays / Thursdays).
The lesson starts at (half past / quarter past) five.

12 **Imagine you hiked yesterday. Draw your route. Then say. (6 points)**

| over | across | near | between ... and ... | around | through | towards | past |

I walked ...

I climbed ...

Score: ___ /18

Whole test score: ___ /80

End of term 3

1 **Read and match. (8 points)**

1 Why are you blushing?	**a** I'm going to go horse-riding.
2 Let's go sailing!	**b** I feel relaxed.
3 What's the matter?	**c** No, I haven't.
4 How do you feel?	**d** Let's give him a present.
5 What makes you feel nervous?	**e** Because I'm embarrassed.
6 Have you got a paddle?	**f** English tests make me feel nervous.
7 What are you going to do tomorrow?	**g** I'm worried.
8 It's John's birthday.	**h** Great idea!

2 **Read and draw. (4 points)**

1 She's crying because she's sad.　**2** A birthday party for John! He feels surprised.　**3** The man is fishing. He's got a fishing rod.　**4** The woman is crazy about surfing.

3 **Read and write. (6 points)**

1 How do you feel? _____

2 What makes you feel proud? _____

3 What are you fond of? _____

4 When do you need a life jacket? _____

5 What are you going to do this weekend? _____

6 What's your family going to do tonight? _____

Score: ____ /18

© Pearson Education Limited 2017　PHOTOCOPIABLE

4 **Look and write. (6 points)**

①

_____

②

_____

③

_____

④

_____

⑤

_____

⑥

_____

5 **Read and write. (12 points)**

> snorkel   embarrassed   rafting   paddle   nervous   bungee jumping   scuba diving
> worried   surfboard   relieved   rock climbing   riding boots

Extreme sports	Emotions	Things

6 **Write about your next family holiday. (8 points)**

I'm going to ...   We're going to ...   I'm fond of/crazy about/scared of ...

My next holiday

_____

_____

_____

_____

_____

_____

_____

Score: ___ /26

7 **Listen and number. (6 points)**

a

b

c

d

e

f

8 **Listen. Then write and match. (8 points)**

1 Timothy feels _____.

2 Elsa feels _____.

3 Cindy feels _____.

4 Katie feels _____.

a  **b**

c  **d**

9 **Look and say. (5 points)**

I feel ... when ...

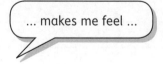
... makes me feel ...

Score: ___ /19

10 **Listen and match. (6 points)**

1 Helen
2 Tom and Harry
3 Gill
4 Fred
5 George
6 Luke and Olga

a  b  c

d  e  f

11 **Listen and write T = True or F = False. (6 points)**

1 Mike is going to go hang gliding next weekend. ☐

He's going to go with his sister. ☐

2 Melissa is going to go scuba diving next week. ☐

She's fond of seahorses. ☐

3 They are going to go kayaking on Sunday. ☐

She needs a fishing rod. ☐

12 **Look and say. (5 points)**

 I'm going to ... next week, so I need ...

Score: ___ /17

Whole test score: ___ /80

1 **Read and circle. (3 points)**

> **John:** What's the matter, Kim?
>
> **Kim:** I'm worried. I have an English test and I'm terrified of tests.
>
> **John:** Don't worry. You're good at English.
>
> **Kim:** Yes, you're right but tests make me feel scared. How about you, John? How are you?
>
> **John:** I'm excited. We're going to the rainforest on holiday next week.
>
> **Kim:** Wow! That's very exciting. What are you going to do?
>
> **John:** We're going to go bungee jumping and we're going to go hiking. I want to see gorillas. But I don't want to see any snakes! I'm scared of snakes. Anyway, good luck with your test.
>
> **Kim:** Thanks. Have fun on your holiday.

1 Kim is
   a   terrified of gorillas.
   b   terrified of tests.
   c   bored of tests.

2 John is
   a   excited.
   b   terrified.
   c   embarrassed.

3 John is scared of
   a   snakes.
   b   the rainforest.
   c   gorillas.

2 **Read and write T = True or F = False. (6 points)**

> I'm Bill. It's summer and I'm on holiday. It's sunny and windy, and the temperature is 20 degrees. We're going to go sailing this afternoon. We often go sailing in the summer on the lake near my house. My mum and dad have got a small boat and I've got my own life jacket.
>
> Yesterday we hiked through the forest. There were many birds. Then we walked across a bridge and to a lake. We could walk around the lake but we couldn't swim across it.
>
> Tomorrow I'm going to play basketball with my friends. It's going to be a lot of fun because I love basketball. I want to be a famous basketball player when I grow up.

1 It's spring. ☐

2 The temperature is 20 degrees. ☐

3 Bill has got a life jacket. ☐

4 Yesterday they hiked in the desert. ☐

5 There were many monkeys. ☐

6 Bill is going to play basketball tomorrow. ☐

3 **Look at Activity 2 and write. (4 points)**

1 What's the weather like today? _____

2 When do they often go sailing? _____

3 Could they swim across the lake? _____

4 What does Bill want to be? _____

Score: ____ /13

1 **Read and write your answers. (7 points)**

1 When do you study English?

_____

2 What's the weather like today?

_____

3 What do you like doing at the weekend?

_____

4 What are you scared of?

_____

5 What are you going to do after school?

_____

6 What makes you feel proud?

_____

7 What do you want to be?

_____

2 **Read and write the questions. (6 points)**

1 _____ She's laughing because she's happy.

2 _____ It was warm and sunny.

3 _____ Tests make me feel nervous.

4 _____ He wants to be a farmer.

5 _____ Monkeys eat bananas.

6 _____ I feel relieved.

3 **Read. Then write about a place where you want to go on holiday. (6 points)**

- Where do you want to go?
- Why?
- What can you see and do there?
- What's the weather like there?

A place to visit

_____

_____

_____

_____

_____

_____

_____

_____

Score: ___ /19

1 Listen and match. (8 points)

is going to go hiking		is going to walk the dog
likes spring	**Julie**	likes autumn
wants to be a ballet dancer	**Ben**	wants to be a builder
is shouting at the dog		is laughing at the dog

2 Listen and circle. (8 points)

1 In spring she loves (listening to / looking at) the birds.
She (likes / doesn't like) autumn.

2 The crocodiles live in a (big / small) lake.
They've also got some (elephants / gorillas).

3 The woman asks about the weather in (spring / winter).
There are usually storms in the (afternoon / evening).

4 He likes the (mornings / evenings).
He (never / always) goes to the park after school.

3 Listen and write T = True or F = False. (4 points)

1 First you go around the lake. ☐

2 Then you go through the forest. ☐

3 Next go along the river and through the waterfall. ☐

4 Then walk for ten minutes. The parrots are in the trees. ☐

4 Listen and tick (✓) or cross (✗). (8 points)

✓ = likes   ✗ = doesn't like

	skateboard	ski	play football	watch films
Pete				
Joanne				

Score: ____ /28

1 **Find five differences. (10 points)**

| under across next to between towards near rainy sunny |
| trees crocodile snake kayak paddle rainforest river |

Picture A

Is/Are there ...?

There is/are ...

I can/can't see ...

Where is/are ...?

Picture B

Score: ___ /10

Whole test score: ___ /70

1 Read and circle. (3 points)

> **John:** What's the matter, Kim?
>
> **Kim:** I'm worried. I have an English test and I'm terrified of tests.
>
> **John:** Don't worry. You're good at English.
>
> **Kim:** Yes, you're right but tests make me feel scared. How about you, John? How are you?
>
> **John:** I'm excited. We're going to the rainforest on holiday next week.
>
> **Kim:** Wow! That's very exciting. What are you going to do?
>
> **John:** We're going to go bungee jumping and we're going to go hiking. I want to see gorillas. But I don't want to see any snakes! I'm scared of snakes. Anyway, good luck with your test.
>
> **Kim:** Thanks. Have fun on your holiday.

1 Kim is

  a terrified of tests.

  b terrified of gorillas.

  c scared of snakes.

2 John is

  a terrified.

  b excited.

  c embarrassed.

3 John is scared of

  a gorillas.

  b snakes.

  c the rainforest.

2 Read and write T = True or F = False. (6 points)

> I'm Katherine. I'm going to stay at my uncle and aunt's house this summer. They live next to the sea and they love sailing. They've got a small boat and they're going to teach me how to sail it. I've got my own life jacket. I'm going to wear a life jacket on the boat.
>
> I often go fishing with my uncle. I don't like fishing but I like looking for crabs. They eat little sea animals and worms. I'm a little scared of big crabs but I like little crabs.
>
> Last summer I visited the desert with my aunt and uncle. It was very warm and sunny! One day it was 38 degrees! We looked at camels and walked to some hills.

1 Katherine lives next to the sea. ☐

2 Her uncle and aunt love sailing. ☐

3 Katherine has got a life jacket. ☐

4 Her uncle likes looking for crabs. ☐

5 Katherine is scared of big crabs. ☐

6 It was humid and windy in the desert. ☐

3 Look at Activity 2 and write. (4 points)

1 What is Katherine going to learn? _____

2 What is Katherine going to wear on the boat? _____

3 What is Katherine scared of? _____

4 Where did they walk to last summer? _____

Score: ____ /13

1 **Read and write your answers. (7 points)**

1 What do you want to be?

_____

2 What do you like doing at the weekend?

_____

3 What was the weather like yesterday?

_____

4 When do you study English?

_____

5 What makes you feel proud?

_____

6 What are you going to do next winter?

_____

7 What are you scared of?

_____

2 **Read and write the questions. (6 points)**

1 _____   I feel relieved.

2 _____   It's 23 degrees.

3 _____   Rock climbing makes me feel scared.

4 _____   No, I don't want to be a journalist.

5 _____   He wants to be a dancer.

6 _____   Monkeys eat bananas.

3 **Read. Then write about a place where you want to live. (6 points)**

- Where do you want to live? Why?
- What can you see and do there?
- What's the weather like there?

A place to live

_____

_____

_____

_____

_____

_____

_____

_____

_____

Score: ____ /19

1   **Listen and match. (8 points)**

is going to walk the dog

is going to go hiking

likes autumn

Ben

likes spring

wants to be a builder

Julie

wants to be a ballet dancer

is laughing at the dog

is shouting at the dog

2   **Listen and circle. (8 points)**

1 In spring she loves (walking in the parks / going on holiday).
She (likes / doesn't like) winter.

2 They've got some (crocodiles / gorillas).
They've also got some (hippos / lions).

3 The woman asks about the weather in (winter / spring).
It's usually (cloudy and humid / sunny and cool) in winter.

4 He (likes / doesn't like) mornings.
He (always / never) goes to the park after school.

3   **Listen and write *T = True* or *F = False*. (4 points)**

1 First you go past the lake. ☐

2 Next you go around the forest. ☐

3 Then go along the river and past the waterfall. ☐

4 Walk for ten minutes. The parrots are in some vines. ☐

4   **Listen and tick (✓) or cross (✗). (8 points)**

✓ = likes   ✗ = doesn't like

	skateboard	ski	play football	watch films
Joanne				
Pete				

Score: ___ /28

1 **Find five differences. (10 points)**

under	across	next to	between	towards	near	sailing	surfing
kayak	paddle	fishing rod	surfboard	happy	bored	sunny	

Picture A

Is/Are there ...?

There is/are ...

I can/can't see ...

Where is/are ...?

Picture B

Score: ___ /10

Whole test score: ___ /70

1 Look and read. Then write. (6 points)

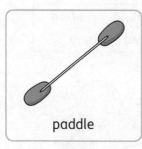

paddle

elephant

thunder

firefighter

bridge

watching TV

1 You use this to kayak. _____

2 I help people. _____

3 You use this to go across a river. _____

4 It lives in grasslands. _____

5 People like doing this in the evenings. _____

6 You hear this after you see lightning. _____

2 Look and read. Then write *Yes* or *No*. (6 points)

1 One boy is surfing. _____

2 Two children are sailing. _____

3 One boy is horse-riding on the beach. _____

4 One girl is fishing. _____

5 One boy is wearing a life jacket. _____

6 The cat hasn't got a paddle. _____

Score: ____ /12

3 **Read and circle the best answer. (4 points)**

Ian is talking to his friend John.

1 **Ian:** Hi, John. You look happy. Why are you smiling?

   John: **a** Because I'm sad.

   b Because I'm going on holiday.

   c Playing basketball makes me feel tired.

2 **Ian:** When are you going?

   John: **a** This weekend.

   b Last summer.

   c I want to go next year.

3 **Ian:** What are you going to do?

   John: **a** I hiked in the rainforest.

   b I hike in the rainforest.

   c I'm going to go hiking in the rainforest.

4 **Ian:** The rainforest. Wow! Do monkeys live in the rainforest?

   John: **a** Yes, they do.

   b They eat fruit.

   c No, I don't.

4 **Read the story. Then write words to complete the sentences. (6 points)**

> I'm Dennis. Next weekend I'm going to go to the mountains with my family. I'm going to stay in a small hut in a forest. The hut is next to a small river and a lake. I'm going to go fishing with my dad. I've got my fishing rod and some worms. We always go fishing in the morning and evening when there are lots of fish. My dog Sandy likes swimming. She often swims towards the fish. They are scared of her and they swim away!

1 Dennis is going to go to the _____ next weekend.

2 The hut is next to a river and a _____.

3 Dennis is going to go _____ with his dad.

4 They _____ go fishing in the morning and evening.

5 Sandy is a _____.

6 The fish are _____ of Sandy.

Score: ___ /10

Listen and draw lines. (5 points)

| Jane | Sam | Phil | Ian | Vicky |

  Listen and write. (5 points)

Wildlife park survey

1 Name: _____

2 Where is the park: near a _____ and a lake

3 Favourite animals: lions and _____

4 Time of lunch: _____

5 Teacher's name: Mr _____

  Listen and draw a line from the day to the correct picture. (4 points)

Where was Charlie last week?

(a)

Monday

(b)

Tuesday

(c)

Thursday

(d)

Friday

Score: ___ /14

4 **Listen and tick (✓). (2 points)**

1 What does Greg want to be?

2 What's Harry going to do tomorrow?

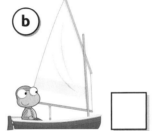

5 **Listen, colour and draw. (5 points)**

Score: ____ /7

1 **Look and read. Then write. (6 points)**

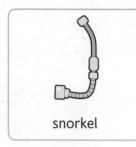
snorkel

crocodile

lightning

police officer

mountain

skateboarding

1 I wear a uniform and help people to be safe. _____

2 You see this before you hear thunder. _____

3 You use this to swim underwater. _____

4 It lives in rivers. It's a carnivore. _____

5 It is bigger than a hill. _____

6 This activity is fun and fast. _____

2 **Look and read. Then write Yes or No. (6 points)**

1 The baby is smiling. _____

2 The dog has got a shirt. _____

3 The birds are eating. _____

4 One man is angry at the dog. _____

5 The man with the sandwich is proud. _____

6 The woman with the bird is happy. _____

Score: _____ /12

3 **Read and circle the best answer. (4 points)**

Myra is talking to her friend Hilary.

1 Myra: What's the matter, Hilary?

   Hilary: **a** She's nervous.

           b I'm tired.

           c I'm smiling.

2 Myra: Why is that?

   Hilary: **a** Because I walked all day yesterday.

           b Because I'm scared of tests.

           c Because he can't sleep.

3 Myra: Where were you?

   Hilary: **a** They were on the coast.

           b She was in the rainforest.

           c I was in the forest.

4 Myra: What was the weather like?

   Hilary: **a** It's sunny and warm.

           b It was warm.

           c It's 23 degrees.

4 **Read the story. Then write words to complete the sentences. (6 points)**

> I'm Susan. Tomorrow it's going to be warm and sunny. I'm going to go to the coast with my family. I love the sea. I'm going to go swimming and snorkelling. My mum has got a small boat and paddles and I've got my snorkel. Last month I practised snorkelling in the swimming pool. I practised every Tuesday and Thursday. The journey to the coast is one and a half hours. There are mountains between my house and the sea. Dad is going to go on a road over the mountain.

1 Susan is going to the _____ tomorrow.

2 She is going to go _____ and snorkelling.

3 Her mum has got a boat and _____.

4 Last month Susan practised snorkelling every Tuesday and _____.

5 It's one and a _____ hours to get to the coast.

6 Susan's house is near the _____ and the sea.

Score: ___ /10

1 Listen and draw lines. **(5 points)**

Vicky	Phil	Jane	Ian	Sam

2 Listen and write. **(5 points)**

Wildlife park survey

1 Name: _____

2 Where is the park: near a forest and a _____

3 Favourite animals: _____ and hippos

4 Time of lunch: _____

5 Teacher's name: Mr _____

3 Listen and draw a line from the day to the correct picture. **(4 points)**

Where was Charlie last week?

a

Monday

Tuesday

b

c

Thursday

d

Friday

Score: ____ /14

4 **Listen and tick (✓). (2 points)**

1 What does Greg want to be?

a  ☐   b  ☐   c  ☐

2 What's Harry going to do tomorrow?

a  ☐   b  ☐   c 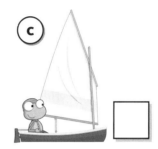 ☐

5 **Listen, colour and draw. (5 points)**

Score: ___ /7

1   **Look at the story. Then say what is happening. (8 points)**

Score: ____ /8

2 Look at the pictures. Say which one is different and why. (8 points)

1  **b**  **c**  **d**

2 **a** **b** **c** **d**

3 **a** **b** **c** **d**

4 **a** **b** **c** **d**
 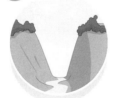  

Score: ___ /8

3 Find four differences. (8 points)

Picture A

Picture B

Score: ___ /8

4 **What do you want to be? Draw a mind map and talk. (8 points)**

Jobs	Reasons

I want to be ...

Useful words	Questions

What do you want to be?

Because I'm good at/I like ...

Why do you want to be a/an ...?

5 **Ask and answer questions. (8 points)**

Topic 1

What do you like/don't you like doing?

Why do you like/don't you like doing it?

When and how often do you do it?

Topic 2

Where did you go last year on your holiday?

What did you do there?

Where are you going to go this year?

What are you going to do there?

Score: ___ /16

Whole test score: ___ /83

Answer Key

Placement

Reading

1 **a** 3 **b** 2 **c** 1 **d** 4

2 **1** do, b **2** Does, a **3** run, d **4** Has, f **5** wearing, c **6** it, e

3 **1** T **2** F **3** F **4** T **5** F **6** T

Writing

1 **1** name **2** nine **3** brother **4** is **5** younger **6** likes

2 (open answers)

3 (open answers)

Listening and speaking

1 Alice: 24, brown

Amy: 9, watching TV

Bill: 19, black, playing the guitar

Tom: 11, 55, skateboarding

2 **1** 19 **2** 15 **3** 20 **4** 80 **5** 14 **6** 70 **7** 30 **8** 16

3 **1** d, g **2** a, h **3** b, e **4** c, f

4 (example answers) There's (a lamp) on (the desk). There's (a guitar) behind (the cat). There's (a bookshelf) above (the bed). There are (books) next to (the lamp). There are (socks) in (the box).

Unit 1

Reading and writing A

1 **1** skateboarding **2** playing computer games **3** watching TV **4** chatting online

2 **1** Does Henry like playing hockey? Yes, he does.
2 Does she like skipping? No, she doesn't.
3 Do your grandparents like skiing? No, they don't.
4 Do you like surfing the internet? Yes, I/we do.

3 **1** doing **2** dog **3** playing **4** guitar **5** magazines **6** cooking **7** like

4 (open answers)

Listening and speaking A

1 **1** b **2** c **3** c **4** a

2 **1** ✓ **2** ✓ **3** ✗ **4** ✗ **5** ✗

3 (example questions and answers) What does he/she like doing? He/She likes (skiing). He/She doesn't like (watching TV). Do they like (walking the dog)? Yes, they do./No, they don't.

Reading and writing B

1 **1** skiing **2** cooking **3** playing the guitar **4** playing computer games

2 **1** Does Willie like walking the dog? No, he doesn't.
2 Do you like surfing the internet? Yes, I do.
3 Does Cindy like riding a scooter? No, she doesn't.
4 Do they like painting? Yes, they do.

3 **1** like **2** chatting **3** playing **4** don't **5** TV **6** likes **7** cooking

4 (open answers)

Listening and speaking B

1 **1** c **2** b **3** a **4** b

2 **1** ✗ **2** ✓ **3** ✓ **4** ✓ **5** ✗

3 (example questions and answers) What do you like doing? I like (skiing). I don't like (watching TV). Do you like (walking the dog)? Yes, I do./No, I don't.

Unit 2

Reading and writing A

1 **1** panda, c **2** monkey, d **3** meat, a **4** fruit, b

2 **1** What do hippos eat?
2 Where do camels live?
3 Where do lions live?
4 What do giraffes eat?
5 What do crocodiles eat?

3 **1** many **2** much **3** have **4** eat **5** run fast

4 (open answers)

Listening and speaking A

1 **1** c **2** a **3** a **4** b

2 ✓ – rainforests, crocodile, river, zebra, desert, camel

3 (example questions and answers) It lives in (rainforests). It eats (leaves). Can it (run fast)? Yes, it can./No, it can't. How much (meat) does it eat? It eats (a lot of meat). Is it (an omnivore)? Yes, it is./No, it isn't.

Reading and writing B

1 **1** hippo, a **2** leaves, c **3** giraffe, d **4** grass, b

2 **1** Where do zebras live?
2 What do pandas eat?
3 Where do crocodiles live?
4 What do birds eat?
5 Where do gorillas live?

3 **1** much **2** swim well **3** many **4** live **5** a lot

4 (open answers)

Listening and speaking B

1 **1** b **2** c **3** c **4** a

2 ✓ – rainforests, crocodile, river, zebra, desert, camel

3 (example questions and answers) It lives in (rainforests). It eats (leaves). Can it (run fast)? Yes, it can./No, it can't. How much (meat) does it eat? It eats (a lot of meat). Is it (an omnivore)? Yes, it is./No, it isn't.

Unit 3

Reading and writing A

1   1 humid   2 wet   3 lightning   4 warm   5 stormy
6 thunder

2   1 What was the weather like last summer?
2 What's the weather like today?
3 What was the temperature yesterday?
4 What's the temperature today?

3   1 F   2 T   3 F   4 F   5 F   6 T

4   (open answers)

Listening and speaking A

1   1 b   2 c   3 a   4 c

2   1 c, spring   2 a, winter   3 b, summer   4 d, autumn

3   (example answers) It was (sunny/warm). It was 30
degrees. She goes water skiing. I (go hiking) in (summer).

Reading and writing B

1   1 temperature   2 stormy   3 warm   4 thunder   5 wet
6 lightning

2   1 What's the weather like today?
2 What's the temperature today?
3 What was the temperature yesterday?
4 What was the weather like last week?

3   1 F   2 F   3 T   4 T   5 T   6 F

4   (open answers)

Listening and speaking B

1   1 a   2 b   3 c   4 b

2   1 d, spring   2 c, winter   3 a, summer   4 b, autumn

3   (example answers) It was (snowy/cold). It was 2 degrees.
He goes skiing. I (go snowboarding) in (winter).

Unit 4

Reading and writing A

1   1 b   2 d   3 c   4 a

2   1 have music lessons   2 mornings   3 quarter to three
4 half past three

3   1 Jane always has piano lessons in the morning.
2 When does Henry do gymnastics?   3 My brother
often learns to cook at midday.   4 What does she do
on Saturdays?

4   (open answers)

Listening and speaking A

1   1 piano   2 mornings   3 afternoons   4 studies
5 Saturdays

2   1 Mondays, 12.00   2 every day, 11.30   3 Wednesday
afternoons, 3.15   4 Saturday afternoons, 4.00
5 every morning, 6.30   6 Tuesday evenings, 6.45

3   (example questions and answers) What activities do
you do? I do (karate). When do you (do karate)? I (do
karate) on (Saturdays). What do you do on (Sundays)?
I (always practise the violin).

Reading and writing B

1   1 a   2 c   3 d   4 b

2   1 do gymnastics   2 afternoons   3 quarter to eleven
4 half past five

3   1 When do you practise the piano?   2 My sister often
studies English in the afternoon.   3 Jack does karate at
four o'clock.   4 When does he learn to draw?

4   (open answers)

Listening and speaking B

1   1 practises   2 Sunday   3 draw   4 evenings
5 gymnastics

2   1 Mondays, 12.00   2 every day, 11.30   3 Wednesday
afternoons, 3.15   4 Saturday afternoons, 4.00
5 every morning, 6.30   6 Tuesday evenings, 6.45

3   (example questions and answers) What activities does
he/she do? He/She (has ballet lessons). When does he/
she (have ballet lessons)? He/She (has ballet lessons) on
(Mondays and Wednesdays). What does he/she do on
(Fridays)? He/She (often goes to parties).

Unit 5

Reading and writing A

1   1 carpenter   2 athlete   3 doctor   4 journalist
5 ballet dancer   6 lawyer

2   1 What, b   2 does, c   3 Does, a   4 want, d

3   1 want   2 basketball player   3 jump   4 helps

4   (open answers)

Listening and speaking A

1   1 ballet dancer   2 wants to be   3 police officer
4 film star

2   1 F   2 F   3 T   4 F   5 T   6 T

3   (example questions and answers) I want to be (an
astronaut) because (I'm crazy about space). I don't want
to be (a singer) because I (can't sing).

Reading and writing B

1   1 firefighter   2 astronaut   3 basketball player
4 film star   5 builder   6 police officer

2   1 do, b   2 does, c   3 want, d   4 be, a

3   1 don't   2 because   3 lessons   4 practise

4   (open answers)

Listening and speaking B

1   1 wants to be   2 film star   3 police officer
4 wants to be

2   1 T   2 T   3 F   4 T   5 F   6 F

3   (example questions and answers) He/She wants to be
(a firefighter) because he/she (likes helping people). He/
She doesn't want to be (an athlete) because he/she
(can't run fast).

Unit 6
Reading and writing A
1 **1** vines, c **2** nest, d **3** valley, b **4** bridge, a

2 **1** walked **2** looked **3** listened **4** climbed **5** stayed **6** played

3 **1** Could they go towards the hills? **2** Could he walk around the mountain? **3** Could she walk around the lake? **4** Could he swim through the river?

4 (open answers)

Listening and speaking A
1 **1** across **2** around **3** through **4** towards **5** waterfall **6** hill

2 **1** over **2** tarantula **3** could **4** lake

3 (example answers) There was a bridge over a river. I walked over the bridge and I climbed down the waterfall. I couldn't jump down. I hiked along the river and walked past two lions.

Reading and writing B
1 **1** waterfall, a **2** vines, b **3** nest, d **4** mountain, c

2 **1** hiked **2** climbed **3** jumped **4** walked **5** looked **6** played

3 **1** Could he swim through the river? **2** Could they go towards the hills? **3** Could he walk around the mountain? **4** Could she walk around the lake?

4 (open answers)

Listening and speaking B
1 **1** bridge **2** mountain **3** through **4** lake **5** past **6** over

2 **1** over **2** tarantula **3** couldn't **4** sea

3 (example answers) I climbed up the waterfall. There was a river. There was a crocodile in the river. I walked over the bridge. Then I hiked around a lake. I walked past two lions.

Unit 7
Reading and writing A
1 **1** blushing **2** shaking **3** crying **4** shouting

2 **1** b **2** d **3** a **4** e **5** c

3 **1** T **2** F **3** F **4** T **5** F

4 (open answers)

Listening and speaking A
1 **1** e **2** a **3** b **4** c **5** f **6** d

2 Al: **1** worried **2** tired **3** surprised **4** relaxed
    Brenda: **1** angry **2** worried **3** surprised **4** relaxed

3 (example answers) I feel (tired). I'm (tired) because (I had a Maths test today).

Reading and writing B
1 **1** yawning **2** blushing **3** laughing **4** shaking

2 **1** d **2** b **3** c **4** e **5** a

3 **1** F **2** T **3** T **4** T **5** F

4 (open answers)

Listening and speaking B
1 **1** b **2** e **3** a **4** f **5** c **6** d

2 Al: **1** worried **2** tired **3** surprised **4** relaxed
    Brenda: **1** angry **2** worried **3** surprised **4** relaxed

3 (example answers) I feel (tired). I'm (tired) because (I had a Maths test today).

Unit 8
Reading and writing A
1 **1** snorkelling, c **2** kayaking, a **3** fishing, b **4** sailing, d

2 **1** b **2** c **3** b **4** a

3 **1** What are you fond of?, I'm fond of rafting. **2** Have you got a paddle?, Yes, I have. **3** Let's go bungee jumping!, Sorry, I don't like bungee jumping. **4** Have you got riding boots?, No, I haven't.

4 (open answers)

Listening and speaking A
1 **1** F **2** T **3** F **4** T

2 **1** beach volleyball **2** rock climbing **3** snorkelling **4** fishing

3 (example questions and answers) What are you (scared of)? I'm scared of (surfing).

Reading and writing B
1 **1** fishing, b **2** snorkelling, d **3** kayaking, c **4** surfing, a

2 **1** b **2** a **3** a **4** c

3 **1** Let's go snorkelling!, Sorry, I don't like snorkelling. **2** Have you got riding boots?, No, I haven't. **3** What are you fond of?, I'm fond of rafting. **4** Have you got a life jacket?, Yes, I have.

4 (open answers)

Listening and speaking B
1 **1** T **2** F **3** T **4** F

2 **1** beach volleyball **2** rock climbing **3** snorkelling **4** fishing

3 (example questions and answers) What are you (scared of)? I'm scared of (surfing).

End of term 1
Reading and writing
1 **1** g **2** c **3** d **4** a **5** h **6** e **7** f **8** b

2 (pictures)

3 (open answers)

4 **1** hippo **2** crocodile **3** zebra **4** snowboarding **5** water skiing **6** hiking

5 Weather: thunder, warm, humid, degrees
    Habitats: desert, grassland, rainforest, forest
    Seasons: autumn, summer, spring, winter

6 (open answers)

Listening and speaking
7 **1** b **2** a **3** c **4** b

8 **1** zebras **2** run fast **3** grass **4** grasslands

9 (example questions and answers) What do you like doing? I like (surfing the internet). Do you like (painting)? Yes, I do./No, I don't. Do your friends like (playing hockey)? Yes, they do./No, they don't.

10 **1** hiking, spring **2** camping, autumn **3** snowboarding, winter **4** water skiing, summer

11 **1** F **2** T **3** F **4** T **5** F

12 (example answer) This is me in winter. I'm (snowboarding). It's (sunny but cold). The temperature is (-2 degrees).

End of term 2
Reading and writing

1 **1** f **2** d **3** h **4** a **5** g **6** c **7** e **8** b

2 (pictures)

3 (open answers)

4 **1** bridge **2** journalist **3** photographer **4** valley **5** mechanic **6** mountain

5 Rainforest: nest, waterfall, vines, hut

Prepositions: over, across, towards, around

Jobs: firefighter, model, astronaut, singer

6 (open answers)

Listening and speaking

7 Mondays, d Tuesdays, b Wednesdays, e Thursdays, c Fridays, f Saturdays, a

8 **1** ballet dancer **2** police officer **3** basketball player **4** astronaut **5** film star

9 (example answers) **1** I always (practise the piano) at weekends. **2** I never (do gymnastics) on Fridays. **3** I want to be (a firefighter). **4** I don't want to be (a ballet dancer).

10 **1** F **2** F **3** T **4** T **5** T **6** F

11 **1** always, photographer **2** climb, valley **3** Tuesdays, quarter past

12 (example answer) I walked (through the forest and towards the waterfall). I climbed (the rock and then I walked over the bridge). I walked (through the river and past the hut).

End of term 3
Reading and writing

1 **1** e **2** h **3** g **4** b **5** f **6** c **7** a **8** d

2 (pictures)

3 (open answers)

4 **1** yawning **2** frowning **3** kayaking **4** snorkelling **5** sailing **6** laughing

5 Extreme sports: rafting, bungee jumping, scuba diving, rock climbing

Emotions: embarrassed, nervous, worried, relieved

Things: snorkel, paddle, surfboard, riding boots

6 (open answers)

Listening and speaking

7 **a** 2 **b** 5 **c** 4 **d** 1 **e** 6 **f** 3

8 **1** relieved, d **2** relaxed, a **3** surprised, c **4** embarrassed, b

9 (example answer) I feel (relaxed) when I (am at the beach). (Singing) makes me feel (nervous).

10 **1** e **2** f **3** a **4** b **5** d **6** c

11 **1** T, F **2** F, T **3** T, F

12 (example answer) I'm going to (go rafting) next week so I need (a paddle).

Final
Reading A

1 **1** b **2** a **3** a

2 **1** F **2** T **3** T **4** F **5** F **6** T

3 **1** It's sunny and windy. **2** They often go sailing in the summer. **3** No, they couldn't. **4** He wants to be a famous basketball player.

Writing A

1 (open answers)

2 **1** Why is she laughing? **2** What was the weather like? **3** What makes you feel nervous? **4** What does he want to be? **5** What do monkeys eat? **6** How do you feel?

3 (open answers)

Listening A

1 Julie: is going to go hiking, likes autumn, wants to be a ballet dancer, is laughing at the dog

Ben: is going to walk the dog, likes spring, wants to be a builder, is shouting at the dog

2 **1** listening to, likes **2** small, elephants **3** winter, afternoon **4** evenings, always

3 **1** T **2** F **3** F **4** T

4 Pete: ✓ skateboard, play football, watch films ✗ ski

Joanne: ✓ watch films ✗ skateboard, ski, play football

Speaking A

(example questions and answers) Is there a (monkey) in picture A/B? Yes, there is./No, there isn't. Are there any (crocodiles) in picture A/B? Yes, there are./No, there aren't. There is a parrot in the trees. There are three trees next to the river. I can see two children. They're kayaking. I can't see a (camel). Where is the snake? It's above the crocodile. Where are the children? They're in the rainforest.

Differences: **1** A = There are no birds in the sky. B = There are two birds in the sky. **2** A = There's no hut. B = There's a hut. **3** A = There's no hippo in the river. B = There's a hippo in the river. **4** A = The boy's got a paddle. B = The boy hasn't got a paddle. **5** = It's rainy. **6** = It's stormy.

Reading B

1 1 a   2 b   3 b

2 1 F   2 T   3 T   4 F   5 T   6 F

3 1 She's going to learn to sail.   2 She's going to wear a life jacket.   3 She's scared of big crabs.   4 They walked to some hills.

Writing B

1 (open answers)

2 1 How do you feel?   2 What's the temperature today?   3 What makes you feel scared?   4 Do you want to be a journalist?   5 What does he want to be?   6 What do monkeys eat?

3 (open answers)

Listening B

1 Julie: is going to go hiking, likes autumn, wants to be a ballet dancer, is laughing at the dog

Ben: is going to walk the dog, likes spring, wants to be a builder, is shouting at the dog

2 1 walking in the parks, doesn't like   2 crocodiles, hippos   3 winter, cloudy and humid   4 doesn't like, always

3 1 F   2 T   3 T   4 F

4 Joanne: ✔ watch films   ✘ skateboard, ski, play football
Pete: ✔ skateboard, play football, watch films   ✘ ski

Speaking B

(example questions and answers) Is there a (surfboard) in picture A/B? Yes, there is./No, there isn't. Are there any (clouds) in picture A/B? Yes, there are./No, there aren't. There's a man. He's got a fishing rod. He's on the rock. I can see a girl sailing. Where is the boy? He's in the kayak.

Differences: 1 A = There's a girl surfing. B = There's a girl sailing.   2 A = The boy's got a paddle. B = The boy hasn't got a paddle.   3 A = There isn't a bird. B = There's a bird.   4 A = The fishing rod is long. B = The fishing rod is short.   5 A = The man is happy. B = The man is bored.

Exam preparation
Reading and writing A

1 1 paddle   2 firefighter   3 bridge   4 elephant   5 watching TV   6 thunder

2 1 Yes   2 No   3 Yes   4 Yes   5 No   6 Yes

3 1 b   2 a   3 c   4 a

4 1 mountains   2 lake   3 fishing   4 always   5 dog   6 scared

Listening A

1 1 film star, Phil   2 ballet dancer, Vicky   3 firefighter, Sam   4 police officer, Ian   5 astronaut, Jane

2 1 Hugh   2 (big) forest   3 hippos   4 one o'clock   5 Thomas

3 Monday, c   Tuesday, b   Thursday, d   Friday, a

4 1 c   2 b

5 1 boat, brown and red   2 girl surfing, black hair   3 draw a big fish in front of the cat   4 draw a balloon above the boy on the horse and write 'adventure camp'   5 draw a dog in the boat and colour it black and white

Reading and writing B

1 1 police officer   2 lightning   3 snorkel   4 crocodile   5 mountain   6 skateboarding

2 1 No   2 No   3 Yes   4 Yes   5 No   6 Yes

3 1 b   2 a   3 c   4 b

4 1 coast   2 swimming   3 paddles   4 Thursday   5 half   6 mountains

Listening B

1 1 film star, Phil   2 ballet dancer, Vicky   3 firefighter, Sam   4 police officer, Ian   5 astronaut, Jane

2 1 Hugh   2 lake   3 lions   4 one o'clock   5 Thomas

3 Monday, a   Tuesday, d   Thursday, c   Friday b

4 1 b   2 c

5 1 boat, brown and red   2 girl surfing, black hair   3 draw a big fish in front of the cat   4 draw a balloon above the boy on the horse and write 'adventure camp'   5 draw a dog in the boat and colour it black and white

Speaking A and B

1 (example answers) 1 It's grandad's birthday. They're having a party. There are lots of people and presents.   2 The girl and her mum are in the kitchen. There's food and a cake. The mum asks the girl to take the birthday cake.   3 The girl is holding the cake. The baby is playing with toys.   4 The girl walks on the toy car. She drops the cake on the floor. The baby is laughing.

2 (example answers) 1 Picture b is different because it's a surfboard. In the other pictures, I can see activities.   2 Picture d is different because it's night time. The other pictures are the seasons.   3 Picture d is different because the hippo is in the water. The other animals are standing.   4 Picture a is different because it's a bridge. The other pictures are of places - a valley, waterfall, mountain.

3 Differences: 1 A = The lion hasn't got any meat. B = The lion's got some meat.   2 A = The boy is wearing white shoes. B = The boy is wearing grey shoes.   3 A = There are leaves in the tree. B = There aren't any leaves in the tree.   4 A = There is no nest in the tree. B = There's a nest in the tree.

4 (example answers) I want to be (an astronaut) because I like (adventures). I want to be (a football player) because I'm good at (football).

5 (example answers)
Topic 1 I like (fishing) because (it makes me feel relaxed). I (go fishing) (every weekend).
Topic 2 Last year I went to (the mountains). I (went hiking). This year, I'm going to go to the (sea). I'm going to go (swimming and snorkelling).

Audioscript

Audio files are available on the Active Teach, or at pearsonelt.com/islands.

M: Man
W: Woman

Placement
Placement Test. Test Booklet. Activity 1. Listen and write.

1

W: Hi. I'm Alice. I'm nine. My favourite number is twenty-four. I've got long brown hair and I like painting.

2

W: Hi. I'm Amy. I'm nine. My favourite number is sixty-two. I've got short, blond hair and I like watching TV.

3

M: Hi. I'm Bill. I'm ten. My favourite number is nineteen. I've got short black hair. I like playing my guitar.

4

M: Hi. I'm Tom. I'm eleven. My favourite number is fifty-five. I've got curly, dark, brown hair. I like skateboarding.

Placement Test. Test Booklet. Activity 2. Listen and circle.

1

W: Nineteen. Nineteen.

2

W: Fifteen. Fifteen.

3

W: Twenty. Twenty.

4

W: Eighty. Eighty.

5

W: Fourteen. Fourteen.

6

W: Seventy. Seventy.

7

W: Thirty. Thirty.

8

W: Sixteen. Sixteen.

Placement Test. Test Booklet. Activity 3. Listen and match.

1

W1: Hi Alice. What do you like doing?

W2: I like chatting online.

W1: When do you chat online?

W2: At the weekend, on Saturdays and Sundays.

2

M1: And Darren, what do you like doing?

M2: I like skiing. I'd like to go skiing every day!

M1: When do you go skiing?

M2: I go with my family in winter.

3

W2: Jo … What do you like doing?

W1: Me? Oh, I like walking the dog with my Mum.

W2: When do you walk the dog?

W1: Well … In the week. I like walking the dog every morning before school.

4

M2: And Alex. What do you like doing?

M1: I like cooking.

M2: Cooking? When do you like cooking?

M1: I like cooking in the evening after school.

Unit 1
Unit 1 Tests A and B. Test Booklet. Activity 1. Listen and circle.

1

M1: What do you like doing in your free time, Robert?

M2: I like skateboarding. I go skateboarding every day after school.

2

W1: Daisy. What do you like doing in your free time?

W2: I haven't got much free time. I like reading books and I like chatting to my friends online.

3

M2: And Jack. What do you like doing in your free time?

M1: I don't like doing much. I'm lazy! I like sitting on the sofa reading or watching TV.

4

W2: Pat. How about you? What do you like doing in your free time?

W1: In my free time … Err … I like … Skiing but that's in winter. I like cooking. Yes. I like cooking. I cook lunch for my family every Sunday.

Unit 1 Tests A and B. Test Booklet. Activity 2. Listen and tick (✓) or cross (✗).

1

W: Tom is at a sports centre. He likes doing exercises. He likes running and climbing. He doesn't like skipping.

2

W: Jo and Sue like drawing and painting. They don't like painting pictures of flowers. They like painting pictures of animals and people.

3

W: Charlie likes playing football. He plays every Tuesday and Thursday after school. He doesn't like the rain … but he always likes playing football!

4

W: Val loves reading magazines. She's got a lot of magazines in her bedroom. She doesn't like reading newspapers. Her Mum and Dad like reading newspapers.

5

W: Tony has got a new bike. He likes riding bikes. His scooter is very old. He doesn't like riding it.

Unit 2
Unit 2 Tests A and B. Test Booklet. Activity 1. Listen and circle.

1

M: This animal is very big. It can run fast and it's strong. It lives in grasslands in Africa. It's grey and hasn't got fur. It's got big ears.

2

W: This animal has got a tail and a long body. It eats meat. It lives on land and in the water. It can swim very fast.

3

M: This animal likes hot countries. It likes forests. It looks for food in the forest. It can climb trees.

4

W: This animal has got a long tail and small ears. It's got light brown fur on its body and dark brown hair on its head. It's called the king of the jungle!

Unit 2 Tests A and B. Test Booklet. Activity 2. Listen and tick (✓) the words you hear.

I'm learning about animals in Africa. This animal lives in rainforests. It's a crocodile. It can swim very fast and it can hide in the river. Then there's the zebra. It's like a horse but it's got black and white stripes. In the Sahara desert there are camels. They are amazing. They've got big feet for the sand and they can walk fast. They can drink a lot of water and can go on long journeys and aren't thirsty! I love learning about animals in Africa.

Unit 3

Unit 3 Tests A and B. Test Booklet. Activity 1. Listen and circle.

1

M: I'm on holiday in Brazil at the moment. It's lovely. I'm at my uncle's and aunt's house. It's great. It's in the rainforest. It's next to the Amazon River. The weather's very warm. It's very rainy too. The afternoons are sunny but the mornings are very warm and wet.

2

M: The temperature isn't too bad. It's not hot. It's about twenty-five degrees after the rain. I don't like very hot weather. I don't like the temperature above thirty degrees.

3

M: We're in the house this morning. There's a big storm outside. There's thunder and lightning and a lot of rain.

4

M: It's a little cooler now. The storm is over and there isn't any rain. The temperature is about twenty-one degrees. There are some clouds in the sky but it's sunny.

Unit 3 Tests A and B. Test Booklet. Activity 2. Listen, match and write.

1

W: Jim and Claire go camping in spring when it's warm.

2

W: Carol goes snowboarding. She goes in winter.

3

W: Pete and Nick love water skiing. They go in summer.

4

W: Pat and Helen go hiking in autumn. They like the colourful leaves!

Unit 4

Unit 4 Tests A and B. Test Booklet. Activity 1. Listen and write.

1

M: What do you do on Wednesdays after school, Jenny?

W: On Wednesdays I practise the piano.

2

M: When do you have your ballet lessons?

W: I have my ballet lessons on Sunday mornings.

3

M: What do you do on Friday afternoons at school?

W: On Friday afternoons I learn to draw.

4

M: When do you study English?

W: I study English on Tuesday evenings.

5

M: And ... what do you do on Saturday?

W: On Saturday I do gymnastics at the sports centre.

Unit 4 Tests A and B. Test Booklet. Activity 2. Listen and match.

1

W: Hi. I have ballet lessons on Monday. They're at lunch time – at midday.

2

W: I study Maths every day. The lesson is at half past eleven.

3

W: I learn to cook on Wednesday afternoons at quarter past three.

4

W: I do karate at the weekend. My lessons are on Saturday afternoons at four o'clock.

5

W: I practise the violin before school. Every morning I practise at half past six.

6

W: I learn to draw with my aunt. She teaches me on Tuesday evenings at quarter to seven.

Unit 5

Unit 5 Tests A and B. Test Booklet. Activity 1. Listen and circle.

1

M1: Hi, Sally. What do you want to be?

W1: Oh, I don't want to be a police officer or a firefighter. I like dancing and acting. I want to be a ballet dancer!

2

M1: What about you, Dan? What do you want to be?

M2: I don't like studying and I don't like dancing or acting. I don't want to be a dancer or a film star. I want to be a police officer.

3

M1: OK. Now Pat. What do you want to be?

W2: I want to be a police officer.

4

M1: And ... what about you, Ben?

M3: I want to be a film star. Everyone wants to be a film star!

Unit 5 Tests A and B. Test Booklet. Activity 2. Read and write T = True or F = False.

1

W1: Hi, Jim. Do you want to be a model?

M1: No, I don't want to be a model! I want to make tables and chairs.

W1: Ah ... you want to be a carpenter, then.

M1: A carpenter? Yes. That's what I want to be!

2

W1: Hi, Paul. Do you want to be a carpenter?

M2: No, I can't make tables and chairs. I want to work with cars and lorries and bikes.

W1: Do you want to be a photographer, then?

M2: Um ... no. I want to be a mechanic. That's what I want to be!

3

W1: Hi, Karen. I want you to be a model.

W2: A model?

W1: Yes. You always want new clothes ...

W2: A model ... mmm. Ok. I want to be a model!

4

W1: And Simon, what do you want to be?

M3: I like music.

W1: Can you sing?

M3: Yes, I can.

W1: Do you want to be a singer?

M3: A singer?

W1: Yes. You can sing and play the guitar!

M3: OK. Why not? I want to be a singer!

5

W1: Now Lucy. Do you want to be an athlete?

W3: No, I don't! I want to take photographs of wild animals.

W1: Ah ... you want to be a wildlife photographer.

W3: Yes. That's what I want to be.

6

W1: OK ... and Pam. What do you want to be?

W4: Er ... I like doing sport. I do sport every day after school.

W1: You want to be an athlete?

W4: No, I want to be an astronaut, just like my hero, Tim Peake.

Unit 6
Unit 6 Tests A and B. Test Booklet. Activity 1. Listen and write.

1

W1: Where is your hut?

W2: My hut ... It isn't very near. Go on this path. There's a big river and a bridge. Go across the bridge.

2

W1: OK. Then?

W2: Then ... there's a big mountain.

W1: Oh no! Do you go over the mountain?!

W2: No, no! I don't go over it. I go around the mountain. There's a path at the bottom.

3

W1: And then ...?

W2: And then I walk next to a small river. There isn't much water in the river so I can walk through the river to the other side.

4

W1: Wow! That's fun!

W2: Then I walk towards the lake.

5

W1: And then ...?

W2: I walk past the waterfall. It isn't very big but it's beautiful.

6

W1: And is that where your hut is?

W2: After the waterfall, there is a small hill. That's before the lake. I go over the hill and you can see my hut from the top.

Unit 6 Tests A and B. Test Booklet. Activity 2. Listen and circle.

1

M1: So ... tell me about your trip. What could you do?

M2: It was fantastic! We could do lots of different activities. We went over a mountain. We could run over it.

2

M2: And we saw a tarantula! It was very big!

M1: Arghh! Were you scared?

M2: Yes. I was scared. It was just behind our hut. I couldn't sleep the first night. But then it was OK.

3

M2: There were lots of birds' nests in the trees. We could hear the birds but we couldn't see them.

4

M1: Could you see the coast?

M2: We could see a lake but we couldn't see the sea. The coast wasn't very near to the hut.

Unit 7
Unit 7 Tests A and B. Test Booklet. Activity 1. Listen and match.

1

M1: What's the matter, Barry?

M2: I'm worried. Today our results come out for the English test.

2

M1: Why are you yawning, Helen?

W1: I'm tired. I went to bed late last night.

3

M1: What makes you feel embarrassed, James?

M3: I'm embarrassed when my teacher wants us to sing in front of the class.

4

M1: Why are you frowning, Sonia?

W2: Ugh. It's my brother. He's got my new bike and I want to ride it. I'm not happy!

5

M2: How do you feel, Gary?

M1: Happy and relieved. I haven't got to go to the dentist today.

6

M1: What makes you feel nervous, Cindy?

W3: I'm not very good at Maths and I get really nervous when we have a test.

Unit 7 Tests A and B. Test Booklet. Activity 2. Listen and circle.

M: My name is Al. I'm worried because I haven't done my homework. Last night I was tired and I didn't do it. This morning I told my mum and she was surprised because I always do my homework. She gave me a letter for my teacher. Now I feel more relaxed!

W: My name is Brenda. I'm angry. My brother listened to my CD. Now he's worried because he can't find it. I was surprised because he usually takes care of my CDs. Mum and Dad are relaxed and are watching TV. I don't want to tell them about this.

Unit 8

**Unit 8 Tests A and B. Test Booklet.
Activity 1. Listen and write *T = True* or *F = False*.**

1

W1: Hey, Eileen. What things are you bored with?

W2: I go fishing every Sunday with my mum and I'm bored with that. We sit for hours for one very small fish! And sometimes we don't catch anything.

2

W1: And, are you scared of anything?

W2: I am scared of scuba diving. I don't like going under the water. And it's cold and dark!

3

W1: And, are you terrified of anything?

W2: Yes. My brother went bungee jumping last month. I went with him but I couldn't jump. I was terrified. He laughed and jumped sixty metres! Arghh! No, thank you!

4

W1: And ... what are you crazy about?

W2: Every year I go sailing with my family. We all love sailing but I'm crazy about sailing. I'm in sailing competitions every weekend.

**Unit 8 Tests A and B. Test Booklet.
Activity 2. Listen and tick (✓).**

1

M: Hey, Tina. What things are you bored with?

W: Umm. I'm bored with beach volleyball. I play every week and we never win!

2

M: And, are you terrified of anything?

W: I don't like walking in the mountains and I'm terrified of rock climbing.

3

M: And, are you scared of anything?

W: Scared? Umm. I don't like swimming in the sea. And I'm scared of snorkelling. Fish look really big when you see them under the water.

4

M: And ... what are you crazy about?

W: Well ... this is a little strange but I'm crazy about fishing. I love fishing. I love sitting by the lake and watching the fishing rod start to move. It's very relaxing. I go every Saturday morning with my dad.

End of term 1

**End of term Test 1. Units 1–3.
Test Booklet.
Activity 7. Listen and circle.**

1

M: What do you like doing in your free time, Sandy?

W: I've got a new computer and after school I like playing computer games. There are lots of new games. It's great!

2

W: Fred. Do you like reading magazines in your free time?

M: No. Not really. I like reading but I don't like reading magazines. I like playing my guitar in my free time.

3

M: And Mary. What do you like doing in your free time?

W: I like doing lots of things. I'm very active. I really like skateboarding. I go every weekend.

4

W: Matt. What about you? What do you like doing in your free time?

M: I really like watching a good film on TV on Friday nights. My friends watch films with me. Fridays nights are pizza and film nights!

**End of term Test 1. Units 1–3.
Test Booklet.
Activity 8. Listen and write.**

Hello. My name's John. I like giraffes and lions, but my favourite animals are zebras. I like zebras because they can run fast. I also like them because they are black and white. Black and white are my favourite colours. Zebras don't eat fruit or meat. They eat grass and they drink water from rivers and from lakes. Zebras live in grasslands, and they don't live in deserts or in rainforests.

**End of term Test 1. Units 1–3.
Test Booklet.
Activity 10. Listen and write.**

1

W: What does Tom like doing?

M: He likes going hiking.

W: When does he go hiking?

M: In spring – when it's warm.

2

M: Do Sally and Lisa like camping?

W: Yes, they do. They go camping in autumn.

3

W: What do John and George like doing?

M: They like going snowboarding.

W: Oh. I like that too!

M: They go snowboarding in winter.

4

M: Does Mary like water skiing?

W: Yes, she does. She goes water skiing in summer.

**End of term Test 1. Units 1–3.
Test Booklet.
Activity 11. Listen and write *T = True* or *F = False*.**

1

W: Hi, I'm Anna. Can you guess my favourite animal? It lives in forests and it eats fruit. It doesn't eat meat and it doesn't sleep a lot. It's not like the lion or the panda. It likes swinging from trees.

2

M: My name's Rob and I live in a special house. It's a boat. We live on a river and I like fishing at the weekend. I like living here.

3

W: Good morning! It was a very cold day yesterday. The temperature was five degrees. But today the sun is out and it's going to be warmer. Right now the temperature is fifteen degrees!

4

M: Hi, Lisa. What do you like doing in your free time?

W: I like watching films about animals in Africa.

M: Do you watch films with your family?

W: I like watching films with my cousin Sarah. But I don't like watching films with my brother. He always says 'I'm bored!'

5

M: Look! These are interesting animals. They live in grasslands in Africa and they like sleeping all day. They're carnivores.

End of term 2
End of term Test 2. Units 4–6. Test Booklet.
Activity 7. Listen and match.

1

M: Do you practise the violin on Mondays?

W: No. On Mondays I practise the piano.

2

M: What do you do on Tuesdays?

W: I do gymnastics on Tuesdays after school.

3

M: What do you do on Wednesdays?

W: I learn to draw on Wednesday afternoons.

4

M: And ... what do you do on Thursdays?

M: I have ballet lessons in the evening.

5

M: What do you do on Friday?

W: I study English on Friday mornings.

6

M: Do you study on Saturdays?

W: No, I do karate on Saturdays.

End of term Test 2. Units 4–6. Test Booklet.
Activity 8. Listen and write.

1

M: Hi, I'm Dan. I don't want to be a police officer or a firefighter. I like dancing. I want to be a ballet dancer.

2

W: My name's Ann. I want to help people. I want to be a police officer. I don't want to be a film star or a ballet dancer.

3

M: I'm Tim. I don't like doing sport so I don't want to be a basketball player. I want to build houses. I want to be a builder.

4

W: Rob, do you want to be a journalist?

M: No, I don't. I want to be an astronaut. I like studying the stars and looking for new planets!

5

M: Claire ... what do you want to be?

W: I don't know. I don't want to be a film star. I like making things. I want to be a carpenter. Yes. That's what I want to be.

End of term Test 2. Units 4–6. Test Booklet.
Activity 10. Listen and write
T = True or F = False.

1

W: Tell me about your trip to the rainforest.

M: There were some vines.

W: Where were they?

M: They were past a big waterfall.

2

W: Wow. What else?

M: We walked to some hills. We walked over a bridge to get to the hills.

W: Were there vines on the hills?

M: Yes, there were.

3

W: Could you swim in the sea?

M: No, we couldn't because it wasn't very near; but we could swim across the river. That was fun.

4

M: And we could swim in the lake.

W: Where was the lake?

M: The lake was between the forest and the hills.

5

W: So ... were you near the mountains?

M: No, not that near. The mountains were towards the coast.

6

W: And were there hummingbirds?

M: Yes, there were. There were some hummingbird nests near our hut. There were four hummingbird nests in the trees.

End of term Test 2. Units 4–6. Test Booklet.
Activity 11. Listen and circle.

1

W: David, tell me. How do you spend your weekends?

M: Well, I like playing computer games and riding my bike. I often go to parties and I always practise the violin.

W: Can you sing?

M: Yes, I can.

W: Do you want to be a singer?

M: Well ... no. I want to be a photographer. I want to take photos of wild animals.

W: Great!

2

M: Hi, Sally. What did you do last weekend?

W: I went to the mountains. I hiked but I couldn't climb to the top.

M: Nice! Did you walk in the forest?

W: No, but I walked through the valley. There were lots of beautiful flowers.

3

M: Jenny, can you play the guitar?

W: No, but I can play the piano. I practise the piano every Tuesday afternoon.

M: What time does your lesson start?

W: It starts at quarter past five and it finishes at half past six.

M: That's a long lesson.

W: Yes. I really like it!

End of term 3

End of term Test 3. Units 7–8.
Test Booklet.
Activity 7. Listen and number.

1

W: Why is Harry frowning?

M: He wants to watch TV but he has to study.

2

W: I'm shaking. There's a big spider in my room!

3

M: I'm blushing because I'm going to sing for my class.

4

W: Stop shouting! I can hear you.

5

W: I'm smiling because it's Friday afternoon! The weekend's here!

6

M: Stop yawning and go to bed. You look so tired.

End of term Test 3. Units 7–8.
Test Booklet.
Activity 8. Listen. Then write and match.

1

W: What's the matter, Timothy?

M: I feel relieved.

W: Really? Why do you feel relieved?

M: Because I passed my English test.

2

M: Why do you feel relaxed, Elsa?

W: Because it's sunny and warm today. I'm at the beach.

3

M: How do you feel, Cindy?

W: I feel surprised.

M: Why do you feel surprised?

W: Because I got a present today. But my birthday is next week!

4

M: What's the matter, Katie?

W: I feel embarrassed.

M: Why? What's wrong?

W: I fell in the playground.

End of term Test 3. Units 7–8.
Test Booklet.
Activity 10. Listen and match.

1

W: Helen has got a mask and a snorkel. She's going to go snorkelling!

2

W: Tom and Harry are crazy about fishing. They've got their own fishing rods.

3

M: Gill, do you want to go sailing?

W: No, I don't like sailing.

M: How about surfing?

W: Yes!

4

W: Hi, Fred. Is this your horse?

M: Yes, it is. Would you like to go horse-riding?

W: Yes, please!

5

M: My brother George loves the sea and he's crazy about kayaking.

6

W: Luke and Olga are my cousins. They were at the lake yesterday and they went sailing.

End of term Test 3. Units 7–8.
Test Booklet.
Activity 11. Listen and write
T = True or F = False.

1

W: Hi, Mike. How was your weekend?

M: Great! I went rafting on Saturday!

W: Wow! And what plans have you got for next weekend?

M: I'm going to go hang gliding.

W: Aren't you scared of flying?

M: No. My sister's scared of flying but I'm not going with her. I'm going with my dad.

W: Great. Have fun!

2

W: My name's Melissa and I'm crazy about the sea. I can swim well and I can surf. I'm going to go scuba diving next month. I'm so excited! I'm going to look at the coral reef and the fish. I'm fond of seahorses.

3

M: Let's go kayaking on Sunday. It's going to be sunny and warm.

W: Can we go sailing instead?

M: No, kayaking is more fun.

W: OK, but I need a life jacket. I haven't got one.

M: Don't worry. I'm going to ask my mum.

Final

Final Tests A and B. Test Booklet.
Activity 1. Listen and match.

1

M: Hi, Julie.

W: Hi, Ben.

M: What are you going to do this weekend?

W: Well, tomorrow I'm going to go hiking in the mountains with my granny and grandad. They're crazy about hiking! On Sunday I'm going to relax. I'm going to watch my favourite programme on TV in the evening. What about you? What are you going to do?

M: I'm going to go to the gym tomorrow. I'm going to do gymnastics. I've got a big competition next month and I want to win! On Sunday I'm going to walk the dog in the morning with my sister and in the afternoon we're going to visit a museum.

2

M: Which months do you like hiking in?

W: I like hiking in autumn. I love walking through the forests and looking at the different coloured leaves. Sometimes it's quite cold but usually the weather is OK. Autumn is my favourite time of the year. Which months do you like walking with your dog?

M: I like walking with my dog in spring. Everything is new. I feel excited about everything. I love walking in the parks. There are new leaves on the trees and the flowers are starting to come out. Spring is my favourite time of the year.

3

W: What do you want to be, Ben?

M: I want to build houses and bridges and important buildings. I want to be a builder. What do you want to be, Julie?

W: I love dancing and music. I want to be a ballet dancer. It's very difficult and you need to practise dancing every day.

4

M: What's the matter? Why are you laughing, Julie?

W: Look at your dog! He's running. He's got your hat! He's bored!

M: Come back here, Billie. Come here!!!

W: Sshhh! You're shouting very loudly!

M: Yes, but ... My hat ... Billieeeeee!

Final Tests A and B. Test Booklet. Activity 2. Listen and circle.

1

M: When is your favourite time of year?

W: I like spring. I love walking in the parks and listening to the baby birds.

M: Do you like autumn?

W: I like the colours in autumn. The leaves change colour and the weather is colder. Yes, I like autumn.

M: What about summer?

W: I love summer. Summer is my favourite time of the year. We go on holiday, it's hot and sunny and everyone is relaxed.

M: And ... Winter?

W: Brrr. No, I don't. I don't like cold weather and the rain!

2

M: What animals are in your wildlife park?

W: We've got some crocodiles. They live in a small lake in the middle of the park. And there's a river next to the lake.

M: Have you got any animals from Africa?

W: We've got some hippos and some elephants.

3

W: OK. Now I'm going to ask you questions. What's the weather like in winter?

M: It's usually very cloudy and humid in winter and there are usually thunder and lightning storms every afternoon.

4

W: And ... When is your favourite time of day?

M: I'm not a morning person. I don't like mornings.

W: What about the evenings?

M: I like the evenings. I can relax and read or watch TV. And I like the afternoons. I always go to the park after school and chat to my friends.

Final Tests A and B. Test Booklet. Activity 3. Listen and write *T = True* or *F = False*.

1

M: Where can you see the parrots?

W: It's not very near. You can go around this lake.

M: And then ...?

2

W: There is a small forest. Go around the forest. Don't go through it because it's dark and there aren't any roads.

3

W: When you are past the forest, there is a river. Go along the river and there is a waterfall. Go past the waterfall.

4

W: After the waterfall, you walk for ten minutes and then you can see some grape vines at the bottom of a hill. Go towards the grape vines. Before the vines there are some trees. The parrots are in those trees. They're beautiful.

Final Tests A and B. Test Booklet. Activity 4. Listen and tick (✓) or cross (✗).

1

M: Joanne. Do you like skateboarding?

W: No, I don't. I'm scared of going fast.

M: What about skiing? Do you like skiing?

W: No. I went skiing last year and I was tired every evening. No, I don't like skiing.

M: Do you like playing football?

W: No. I don't like football. I don't like ball games.

M: Oh ... OK ... And ... What about films? Do you like watching films?

W2: I'm crazy about films. I watch a new DVD every day. I go to the cinema every Friday and Saturday with my friends and we watch all the new films. It's great!

2

W: Pete. What do you like doing? Do you like skateboarding?

M: Yes, I love skateboarding. I go after school every day.

W: Do you like skiing?

M: No. I never go skiing. I don't like cold weather.

W: Do you like playing football?

M: I like playing football when it's warm and sunny.

W: And ... Do you like watching films?

M: I watch DVDs at home. I love scary films.

Exam preparation
Exam preparation Tests A and B. Test Booklet.
Activity 1. Listen and draw lines.

1

M: Can you see the man with the sunglasses?

W: Yes. Is he a film star?

M: Yes. His name is Phil.

2

M: There is a girl dancing.

W: Is she a ballet dancer?

M: Yes, she is. Her name is Vicky.

3

M: OK. Now, there is a man with a helmet on his head.

W: The firefighter?

M: Yes. His name is Sam.

4

M: Now. Can you see the police officer?

W: The man wearing a uniform?

M: Yes. That's him.

W: What's his name?

M: His name is Ian.

5

M: OK. Can you see the woman in the space suit?

W: The astronaut?

M: Yes. That's her. Her name's Jane.

Exam preparation Tests A and B.
Test Booklet.
Activity 2. Listen and write.

1

W: Hello. I want to ask you some questions about the wildlife park you are going to next week. First, what's your name?

M: My name's Hugh.

W: H-U-G-H?

M: Yes, that's right.

2

W: Where is the wildlife park?

M: It's near a big forest and a lake.

W: Is it in this country?

M: Yes, it is. I'm going with my class on a school trip.

3

W: What are your favourite animals?

M: I love lions and hippos best.

W: What animals are in the wildlife park?

M: There are some lions and some giraffes and lots of monkeys.

4

W: What time are you going?

M: We're going at half past nine.

W: Are you going to have lunch in the park?

M: Yes. We're going to have lunch at one o'clock.

5

W: What's the name of your teacher?

M: Mr Thomas.

W: Is that T-H-O-M-A-S?

M: Yes. That's right.

W: Thanks. Have a great day!

Exam preparation Tests A and B.
Test Booklet.
Activity 3. Listen and draw a line from the day to the correct picture.

Where was Charlie last week?

1

W: Hi, Charlie. Where were you last week?

M: Well ... on Monday I was doing gymnastics. I was at the gym.

W: Do you like gymnastics?

M: Yes, I love gymnastics. I go to the gym every day.

2

W: And ... what about Tuesday?

M: On Tuesday ... I was dancing. I love ballet dancing and I have my ballet lesson every Tuesday.

W: What time is your ballet lesson?

M: It's after school at half past four.

3

W: And ... what about Wednesday?

M: On Wednesdays, I relax. But on Thursday, I was at karate.

W: What belt are you?

M: I'm a brown belt.

4

W: And ... what about Friday. Where were you on Friday?

M: I was at home. I've got a piano exam in two weeks and I practise every morning before school.

Exam preparation Tests A and B.
Test Booklet.
Activity 4. Listen and tick (✓).

1

What does Greg want to be?

W: What do you want to be Greg?

M: I don't want to be a policeman.

W: Oh ...?

M: I don't like uniforms!

W: What about a dancer?

M: I love dancing. But I don't want to be a dancer. I want to be an astronaut and go into space!

2

What's Harry going to do tomorrow?

W: So, Harry. What are you going to do tomorrow?

M: Is it Saturday tomorrow?

W: Yes.

M: Then, I'm going to read in bed before breakfast.

W: And then what are you going to do?

M: Umm ... on Saturday I usually go fishing with my dad but tomorrow a friend is going to go sailing. I'm going to go with him. So ... I'm going to go to the coast for the day and we're going to go sailing.

W: Have fun!

M: Thank you!

Exam preparation Tests A and B.
Test Booklet.
Activity 5. Listen, colour and draw.

1

W: Hi, Oliver. Look at this picture. What's in the picture?

M: There are people doing different activities.

W: Yes. That's right. Can you see the girl in the boat?

M: The girl with the spiky hair?

W: Yes. That's her. I want you to colour her boat brown and red.

2

W: OK. Now can you see the girl at the front of the picture?

M: The girl surfing?

W: Yes.

M: Can I colour her hair black?

W: Yes, you can.

3

W: OK. Now I'd like you to draw something for me. Can you see the girl with the fishing rod?

M: Yes. She's wearing a hat.

W: Can you see the cat behind her?

M: Yes.

W: Can you draw a big fish in front of the cat?

M: OK. There.

4

W: OK. Now I'd like you to write something for me. Can you see the picture of the boy horse-riding?

M: Yes, he's riding on the beach. He's riding towards the cat.

W: Yes. That's the one. I want you to draw a balloon above his head and write 'Adventure Camp' on the balloon.

M: That's A-D-V-E-N-T-U-R-E then C-A-M-P.

W: Yes, that's right.

5

W: OK. In front of the girl in the boat, I want you to draw a dog.

M: What colour is the dog?

W: You can choose.

M: OK. It's a black and white dog.

W: Great. Thank you.

Evaluation chart

PUPIL'S NAME	EVALUATION CHART								
	Placement	1	2	3	4	5	6	7	8

MARKING CRITERIA: ★ = Still developing   ★★ = Progressing well   ★★★ = Excellent

Evaluation chart

PUPIL'S NAME	EVALUATION CHART				
	End of term 1	End of term 2	End of term 3	Final	Exam preparation

MARKING CRITERIA: ★ = Still developing ★★ = Progressing well ★★★ = Excellent

Pearson Education Limited
Edinburgh Gate
Harlow
Essex CM20 2JE
England
and Associated Companies throughout the world.

Poptropica® English Islands

First published 2017
Second impression 2017
ISBN: 978-1-2921-9868-2

Set in Fiendstar 12/14pt
Printed in Neografia, Slovakia

Acknowledgements: The publisher would like to thank Kerry Powell and
Katie Foufouti for their contributions to this edition.

Illustrators: Humberto Blanco (Sylvie Poggio Artists Agency), Anja
Boretzki (Good Illustration), Chan Cho Fai, Lee Cosgrove, Leo Cultura,
Marek Jagucki, Jim Peacock (Beehive Illustration), Mark Ruffle (The
Organisation), and Yam Wai Lun

Picture Credits: The publisher would like to thank the following for their
kind permission to reproduce their photographs:

(Key: b-bottom; c-centre; l-left; r-right; t-top)

123RF.com: stockbroker 42c, Cathy Yeulet 42l; **Alamy Stock Photo:**
Image Source Plus 42r

All other images © Pearson Education

Every effort has been made to trace the copyright holders and we
apologize in advance for any unintentional omissions. We would be
pleased to insert the appropriate acknowledgement in any subsequent
edition of this publication.

ISBN 978-1-292-19868-2